D1543278

BOTANICAL ORCHIDS

and how to grow them

BOTANICAL ORCHIDS
and how to grow them

JACK KRAMER

GARDEN • ART • PRESS

Frontispiece: *Laelia cinnabarina*
Endpapers: *Paphiopedilum argus*

British Library Cataloguing-in- Publication Data
A catalogue record for this book is available from the British Library

Printed in England
by the Antique Collectors' Club, Woodbridge, Suffolk
on Consort Royal Era Satin paper
supplied by the Donside Paper Company, Aberdeen, Scotland.

∼ CONTENTS ∼

Dendrobium farmeri

～ INTRODUCTION ～

Recently, there has been a new interest in an old subject: botanical or species orchids as they are otherwise known. These orchids are straight from nature, the product of natural evolution.

In this specific context the word botanical or species is used in contrast with the word hybrid. For the sake of clarity in this book we use the word species in its common senses only to refer to groups of related plants belonging to a genus.

The environmental movement has spawned this renaissance of attention, aided by the growers' ability to propagate these plants by cloning using the meristem system. The resultant saving of botanical orchids is crucial since the natural habitat of many orchids is being plundered.

Hybrid orchids are the offspring from the cross between two different species. The manmade hybrids of Cattleyas and Phalaenopsis available to the public now number in the thousands and there are many books about them. Here they are only covered peripherally. The botanicals, on the other hand, offer a unique selection for the hobbyist and collector.

The word orchid is used to describe the vast Orchidaceae family. There are more than 35,000 different species of botanical orchids, 1,600 alone in the Dendrobium genus. Orchids are termed as terrestrial – growing in the ground – or epiphytic – growing on trees or rocks (technically called xerophytic on rocks). They do not feed from their host in the manner of a parasite but draw moisture and nourishment from rain and humus. Some orchids are from tropical zones but many are from temperate zones as well.

Orchids are classified as sympodial or monopodial. Sympodial orchids bear a new growth each year from the base of the preceding growth; this produces flowers, makes its roots, and the cycle is repeated. In the other type of growth – monopodial – there is one stem that grows taller each year and there is no new shoot from the base of the plant. Flower spikes and roots grow from the leaf axils.

Some orchids mentioned here may be somewhat difficult to locate but I have included a list of suppliers both here and abroad.

The colour photos and concise text will help you grow the fine botanicals (I discuss over 350 species) and enable you to join the league of collectors. So here once again, three decades after my first book on orchids, I hope to further interest in the gems of the orchid world – the botanicals.

∼ ACKNOWLEDGEMENTS ∼

I wish to thank the many friends and orchid growers both in the U.K. and the U.S.A. that have in one way or another helped me in the process of doing this book. There were many, but special gratitude goes to Mrs Fordyce Marsh who contributed many photos taken from her past trips to foreign lands. And thanks to Jeff Corder of Ft Myers, Florida, who shared his photos and knowledge with me. In addition there were many orchid growers who answered my questions freely both in the United Kingdom and in the United States: Hausermann Orchids, Oak Hill Orchids, Carter & Holmes Orchids and also thanks to Longwood Gardens in Pennsylvania and Strybing Arboretum in San Francisco.

And surely I owe many thanks to Brian Cotton of the Antique Collectors' Club of England and to Diana Steel who thought enough of my idea to visit me in the U.S.A. and who also contributed photos.

This book has been four years in the making and I have probably forgotten some people that should be mentioned so apologies if so.

And lastly, as always, my thanks to the wonderful world of orchids – flowers I have grown for almost thirty years in all types of climates. They have brought an incredible amount of joy to my life and I hope through this book to share that pleasure with you.

Jack Kramer
Naples, Florida
March 1998

∼ ORCHID NAMES ∼

Botanical names of orchids change. In this book I have opted for the most popular name of the orchids as listed in catalogues and in general usage. For this, I request your tolerance. I have always been a hands-on gardener and have not delved into the depths of orchid taxonomy.

The names of botanical orchids (the orchids which are largely dealt with in this book) are normally composed of two parts.

First comes the name of the genus (pl. genera) which embraces closely related individual species. Examples of genus names are Cattleya, Dendrobium and Vanda. Individual species within a genus are identified by a second name attached to the genus name. Examples of species names are *Cattleya bicolor*, *Dendrobium formosum*, and *Vanda merillii*. Species names are chosen in many ways; *Cattleya bicolor* is named after the colour of the flower, *Dendrobium formosum* after the geographical location and *Vanda merillii* after the plantsman's name. These names are always italicised, the genus name begins with a capital letter and the species name is entirely in lower case.

The nomenclature for orchids that have been hybridised is different. A hybrid is an orchid that has been mated with another orchid or two other orchids to produce a new plant or cultivar/variety. The name of the new cultivar is always enclosed in quotation marks. For example *BLC Acapana* 'Miles' (where B stands for Brassia, L for Laelia and C for Cattleya).

Orchid names change as time goes on and taxonomists rename certain genera on new findings. For example, many Epidendrums are now called Encyclias and some Odontoglossums are called Rossioglossum.

Generally, I have tried to place plants in their genus as they are accepted by most growers and are listed in growers' catalogues. I have used widely accepted names instead of trying to define borderline species that still puzzle taxonomists.

As a general rule to plant spelling I have used the Royal Horticultural Society's *Dictionary of Gardening* (four volumes) published by The Clarendon Press, Oxford in 1965. Recently this work has been updated and revised.

The mystique of orchids is well illustrated in this drawing of Zygopetalum rostratum *by the botanical artist John Nugent Fitch who worked thousands of plates for* Curtis's Botanical Magazine *in the late* 1800s

∼ CHAPTER 1 ∼
The Mystique of Orchids

For over one hundred years, ever since their immense popularity in England, orchids have been called 'exotic' – strangely beautiful, enticing. The mystical attitudes and feelings surrounding these plants persist today.

No flower has been as maligned or as revered as the orchid since its first appearance centuries ago. Orchids have through the ages been called Flowers of Satyr (Satan), Flowers of Sexual Prowess, Flowers of the Four Seasons, parasites, and have been depicted as cannibalistic. All wrong.

Royals were the first to cultivate the plants; they alone could afford the orchid which became a status symbol. Scientifically, the orchid is the most advanced plant we know in the plant kingdom, quite unlike other plants, and this increases its allure. The secret of the mystique of orchids is clothed in time and the legend and lore that surrounds them captivates the imagination. These are truly plants of infinite beauty and magic.

Although Europe is considered the home of the orchid cult that began in the eighteenth century, orchids were cultivated in the Orient long before then. In the 28th century B.C., *Bletilla hyacinthina* and a Dendrobium were described in various Chinese manuscripts. It was what the Chinese philosopher Confucius (551-479 B.C.) called the *Lan* (fragrance) of the orchid flowers that attracted the Chinese people to the plants.

Centuries later, Chinese paintings from the Yuan Dynasty (1279-1368) depicted the beauty of the tapered grass-like leaves of Cymbidiums. Orchids were also cultivated in Japan; Engelbert Kaemper, a German doctor working for the Dutch Trading Company, referred to the orchids he noticed in Japan in the mid-seventeenth century. Orchid books began appearing in Japan in 1728; *Igansai ranpin*, published in 1772, described Cymbidiums, Aerides, Dendrobiums, and other orchids. The mystique of the orchid thrived in Japan, where royal families and feudal lords doted on the orchids they cultivated.

Orchids for medicinal use
Orchids in the western hemisphere were first used for medicinal purposes. In the first century A.D., Dioscorides, a Greek physician, wrote *De Materia Medica*, in which he described five hundred plants, including two orchids that he declared sexual stimulants because the orchid tubers resembled testicles. It was thus thought that orchids contributed to fertility and virility. During the Middle Ages, the

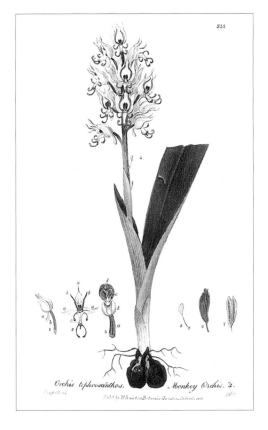

Ever since the days of herbal manuscripts the orchid was associated with sex because the tubers of some orchids resembled testicles, as shown in this illustration of Orchis tephrosanthes *(Monkey orchid) by Isaac Russell from Baxter's* Botanic Garden, *1837*

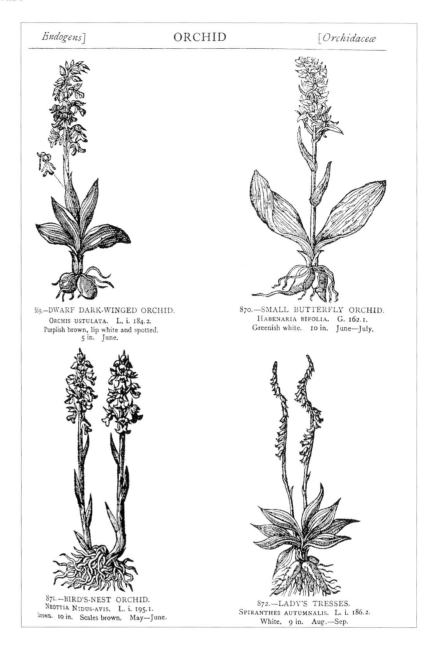

Native orchids portrayed mainly for identification for medicinal purposes, from Peter P. Good's The Family Flora and Materia Medica Botanic, 1847. *The drawings show the beginning of botanical art progressing from identification to decorative art*

Doctrine of Signatures was postulated, attributing the preparations of certain orchids with the ability to help produce male offspring.

In 1552, the Aztec Badianus Herbal depicted Vanilla, an orchid. Vanilla appeared again between 1571 and 1577 when Francisco Hernandez of Spain discovered it in Mexico and in 1605 in the work of Clusius (Carolus). Also in the Middle Ages, the herbals of John Gerard and John Parkinson, published in 1597 and 1629 respectively, considered orchids important for their usefulness to humans.

Describing orchids

In 1703, *Hortus Indicus Malabaricus,* by H.A. Rheede tot Draakenstien (1636-1691), the Dutch governor of Malabar in India, was published. Draakenstien, a botanist by training, wrote about the many orchids of tropical Asia, including Rhyncostylis, Dendrobiums, Vandas, and Cymbidiums. G.E. Rumphius, a clerk employed by the Dutch East India Company, was the first person to discover and subsequently describe Phalaenopsis (then called Angraecum). And in 1687, Hans Sloane

Orchids growing on tree limbs, a fairly true rendition of epiphytic orchids. From a German publication of 1890

discovered orchids in Jamaica. Mention of the first tropical orchid cultivated in Europe appeared in Paul Hermann's *Paradisus Batavus* (1698); it was an Epidendrum orchid from Curacao and was introduced in Holland.

In the eighteenth century, botanical science was born, along with the first attempts at plant classification. The great Swedish botanist Linnaeus introduced systematic botany in his *Genera Plantarum* (published in 1737), placing orchids in classes founded on the number and positions of the stamens and pistils of the flowers. In 1753 he described eight orchid genera; in 1763 he published another treatise in which he named one hundred different species, but he placed all the species within the same genus: Epidendrum. In 1825 the Dutch botanist Karl Ludwig Blume really established the species, describing orchids in his many works.

The English love affair
The eighteenth century also saw the beginning of the English love affair with orchids. In 1731 the first tropical orchid to flower in England was *Bletia purpurea (verracunda)*,

Dendrobium nobile. *Dendrobiums are a popular orchid.*

Angraecum leonis, *a small flowered Angraecum with flowers like birds on a perch. Cool growing.*

which had been sent from New Providence Island in the Bahamas to the famous collector Peter Collinson. Linnaeus called the orchid *Limodorum tuberosum*. By 1737, some North American orchids had appeared in England; Philip Miller, in his *Gardener's Dictionary*, described *Cypripedium parviflorum (pubescens)*, called Helleborine. Dr. John Fothergill was the first European to collect Asiatic orchids; he brought back *Phaius grandifolius* and *Cymbidium ensifolium* from China in 1778.

In these early years of orchid collecting, orchids mesmerised the English

From Pflanzenleben *by Anton Kerner von Marilaun, published in 1890 in Leipzig, a typical picture of a tropical environment where orchids grow. The watercolourist has taken many liberties with epiphytes growing in the ground*

'Orchid House in the Natural Style'. Dated 1874, this is a fascinating engraving, for it illustrates not only the passion of the times for orchids, but also the 'natural' arrangement considered to be ideal. Frontispiece from F.W. Burbidge's Cool Orchids and How to Grow Them, *1874*

people. The Royal Botanic Gardens of Kew, England, was originally a nine-acre garden started in the grounds of the Dowager Princess of Wales and remained a private garden for eighty-two years. Vanillas and Epidendrums were imported from the West Indies; by 1768, the garden had twenty-four orchids, most from the West Indies but also some British species and Cymbidiums and Phaius from China. Aiton's *Hortus Kewensis* (1789) mentions orchids at Kew Gardens. By 1813 Kew Gardens had eighty or so orchids, mainly then called Epidendrums. In 1841 the garden passed into the hands of the British government, with Sir William Hooker, a professional taxonomist and botany professor at the University of Glasgow, becoming its first director.

Orchids were difficult to collect, and plant-hunting expeditions were fraught with danger and the unexpected. Lurid tales of naked natives adorned with orchids added to the mystique of the plants. Countries such as Borneo, Sumatra, New Guinea, Burma, Ecuador, Colombia and Costa Rica were unknown lands, and flowers from these areas carried the touch of enchantment people wanted in their lives. Various establishments and notable people contributed to the ever-growing interest in orchids. The Horticultural Society of London, founded in 1809, helped fan the interest at its gardens in Chiswick. During this time, *Curtis's Botanical Magazine* featured many exotic orchid species. Conrad Loddiges & Sons opened their Hackney nursery about 1812. Loddiges' twenty-volume publication, the *Botanical Cabinet* (finished in 1833), became a guide post to the cultivation of orchids.

Cattleya orchids, popular all over the world and the prototype orchid as people know the genus

Cattleyas in a lath house where the trellis type construction affords protection from strong sunlight

Orchids growing in a screened enclosure where they are subject to natural rainfall. These enclosures are popular in all year temperate climates

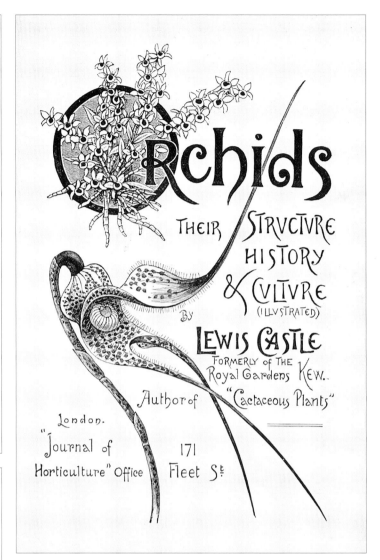

This advertisement for B.S. Williams' book The Orchid-Growers' Manual *shows just how popular it was, for here it is in its '6th edition, enlarged and revised'. It was first published in 1852*

Orchids, Their Structure, History and Culture *by Lewis Castle. This orchid 'how-to' book was first published in London in 1887. More than a hundred years later it is still an excellent source of information on orchids*

The enterprising and famous dynasty of Veitch owned the Royal Exotic Nursery in Chelsea, from which came many new orchids for the conservatories of Victorian England

The interior of a typical orchid house in the latter half of the 19th century when the love affair with foreign plants blossomed in the greenhouses of England, orchids being the prized plants. An engraving from The Orchid Growers' Manual, *7th edition, 1894*

Orchid collecting became so intense that the plants were actually used as packing materials for other tropical plants sent to William Cattley. The genus Cattleya was named for Cattley; it caused a sensation when it was introduced because of its unusual flower: a large lip. Dr. Lindley, the secretary of the Royal Horticultural Society and editor of the *Gardener's Chronicle*, received many new orchids and became an authority on many species. In 1830 Lindley issued rules for the cultivation of orchids (although later research proved that high temperature and humidity are not always the ingredients for growing orchids). The Duke of Devonshire had a vast collection of orchids at Chatsworth; his caretaker, Joseph Paxton, was responsible for maintaining the collection and he furthered the mystique of orchids. (Paxton was the one who disproved Lindley's dictum about high temperature and high humidity.) Earl Fitzwilliam also had a reputable collection at Wentworth.

Robert Warner and his gardener Ben Williams are famous names among orchid lovers. Warner's *Select Orchidaceous Plants* (3 vols, 1862-4) is a fund of information. Williams founded the firm of B.S. Williams & Son at Holloway, specialising in orchids, and his *The Orchid-Grower's Manual* is still a standard work in orchid culture. Messrs. James Veitch & Sons, who ran the Royal Exotic Nurseries at Kings

Dendrobium chrysotis (now D. chrysotoxum) *as depicted in Lucien Linden's famous* Lindenia *or* Iconography of Orchids, *1855-1902*

Humming-birds pollinating orchids in a plate by the famous and prolific 19th century ornithological artist John Gould

Bulbophyllum carinatum *from Lucien Linden's* Lindenia

'The Phalaenopsis House at Oldfield, Bickley'. The engraving appeared in The Journal of Horticulture, *1887*

Road in Chelsea, and F.H. Sander, of St. Albans, Hertfordshire, greatly furthered the dispersal of information about the cultivation of orchids.

Various orchid lovers had trouble cultivating orchids because no one knew the native growing conditions of the hundreds of plants from foreign lands flooding the European market courtesy of collectors such as Roezl and Skinner. A map of a stand of orchids, indicating altitude, the exact growing area, and other pertinent topographical facts, was valued more than a treasure map, such was the demand in the late 19th century. Between 1840 and 1890, orchid collecting became what today we call a mania. Orchids took all of Europe by storm and were considered elegant, dignified, and a symbol of wealth, the flowers of royalty. The orchid replaced other plants in the homes and conservatories of the people. Some Victorian collections numbered 10,000 orchids (so much for my paltry indoor garden of three hundred!). The explosion of the popularity of orchids led to a need for housing for the plants: the greenhouse was born, pioneered by Joseph Paxton, famous for the Crystal Palace, constructed in 1851. The classic florilegium J. Bateman's *Orchidacea of Mexico and Guatemala* (1837-41), with exquisite handcoloured plants rendered by Augusta Withers and other artists, perfectly captured the mood of the time.

More florilegia flooded the market as demand for information about orchids increased. Warner's *Orchid Album* and Lucien Linden's *Lindenia* were notable, with stunning pictures on vellum. The artists of the day depicted the orchids in such depth that their works wore a mantle of even greater beauty than the plants themselves. Such volumes created even more interest in orchids, and great parties and fêtes were held to celebrate the blooming of the phenomenal plants.

Orchids in America

It was in the 1830s that Americans became enamoured with orchids. At an 1837 meeting of the Massachusetts Horticultural Society, an Oncidium was exhibited, while the following year, John Wright Booth, a collector in Boston, received plants. In New England, especially, the people were fascinated with orchids. For the next decade Oncidiums were mainly the orchids cultivated; by 1856 Messrs. Low of England were shipping various orchids to Edward S. Rand, a fervent orchid fancier. Other collections thrived in Boston and the New York area.

Harvard University had the good fortune to have Professor Oakes Ames in its employ; Ames became an orchid authority renowned throughout the world. For more than forty years he studied orchids and described them in his assorted writings. Harvard became the Mecca of orchidology in the United States. When Ames died, his collection was bequeathed to the university and subsequently acquired by the American Orchid Society in West Palm Beach, Florida, USA.

Although orchids were quite popular, it was not until 1920 that the American Orchid Society was formed, at the Horticultural Hall in Boston. The Society's bylaws were established at the American Museum of Natural History in New York in 1921. For the next decade the membership was small, but in 1931 quarterly bulletins were funded and the American Orchid Society became successful. In June 1940 the bulletins began being published monthly by Dr. Louis Williams, assisted by Gordon Dillon. Dillon was appointed executive secretary of the Society, and the popularity of orchids grew even more. In 1954 the first World Orchid Congress was held in St. Louis at the Missouri Botanical Gardens. In 1996 the World Orchid Congress was held in Rio de Janeiro, Brazil.

At first Americans were solely interested in the botanical orchids, deriving much pleasure from the fascinating Laelias, Chysis and Angraecums. By the 1960s, orchids, once considered hard to grow and only for the well-to-do, became affordable and available to everyone, because of meristem culture. Mail order houses such as Hausermann's proliferated as crops of carnations gave way to orchids. Many growers of cut flowers turned their establishments into veritable orchid farms.

Orchids today

The decades of the 1970s and 1980s ushered in a fascination with the countless hybrid orchids, the Cattleyas, Cypripediums, Phalaenopsis, and on and on. Hybrids by the thousands were registered by growers with the Royal Horticultural Society in London, and Cattleyas of all colours but black led the way, with their exquisite pastel shades. The Phalaenopsis, a species of a beautiful white tone, was hybridised into a carnival of colour, from yellow and pink, candy-striped, blotched, and spotted. The long wands of gorgeous long-lasting flowers spaced evenly on graceful arching stems were highly prized. But, by the 1990s, orchid lovers had become tired of the abundance of form and colour; hybridisation had reached overkill.

Phalaenopsis schilleriana. *From Favourite Flowers of Garden and Greenhouse, E. Step and W. Watson, 1897.*

Vanda tricolor. *From Favourite Flowers of Garden and Greenhouse, E. Step and W. Watson, 1897.*

Vandas and Ascocendas growing in a conservatory. These plants do well with artificial heat and need much sunlight

Orchids exhibited at a flower show

An orchid grower's Phalaenopsis house where these popular orchids bloom profusely

I still remember the thrill I felt when I saw my first *Vanda coerulea*, a botanical orchid also known as the Blue Orchid, bloom in my solarium in Chicago in 1961. The grower I bought it from was reluctant to sell it to me; he gave me the plant's history in return for my paying his high price. Sir Joseph Dalton Hooker of Kew Gardens claimed he first discovered the Vanda in Assam in 1837, growing high in the mountains. The blue colour of the plant was stunning. Hooker collected more than 250 species of orchids; his *Himalayan Journal* chronicled the events.

Even then, about 1880, lands were being plundered, as they are today, but the governments of Assam and Burma soon put a strict limit on how orchids could be collected. At the end of the twentieth century the ransacking of South American rain forests, however, for orchids was horrific: thousands of trees were felled so people could get to the arboreal orchids. One intrepid explorer and collector reported 4,000 trees felled, 1,200 orchids collected. In England, one orchid plant could bring 1,000 guineas. In the 1970s many of the homelands of orchids around the world were destroyed as the trees the orchids lived in were cut down for lumber, for development, and for the orchids themselves. I still recall visiting a commercial grower in 1967 and seeing a shipment of orchids from Thailand being unpacked – here were hundreds of orchids direct from the jungle, and the thrill of having a few in my collection was my main interest.

Fortunately, I learned better, as have many countries that are trying to restrict destruction and trying to save the remaining orchid species by limiting the exportation of these prized plants, and thus ensuring the beauty of the orchids for future generations. Commercial growers, via sophisticated methods, are preserving the botanical orchids. The Mormodes, the Pleurothallis, and the Anguloa, and all the available species, are providing orchid collectors everywhere with the rare, the beautiful, and the unusual.

Vanda orchids in Costa Rica.

∼ CHAPTER 2 ∼
The Orchid: Its Structure and How It Grows

Orchids are flowering plants of the family Orchidaceae. They are either monocotyledons – having a single seed leaf upon germination, or dicotyledons – having a pair of seed leaves. The orchid has a diverse appearance; whereas a rose looks like a rose, an orchid can look like a tulip, a tiny chrysanthemum, a spider, and so on. The structures of the orchid flowers and leaves are equally diverse, with the lip often an extended petal and the leaves leathery (Brassavolas) or paper thin (Sobralias).

Monopodial Orchids
Some orchids are monopodial, growing in one continuous direction. The stems lengthen season after season, as though they are slowly crawling; aerial roots have a lateral inflorescence produced from the axils of the leaves or opposite the axils. The roots become flattened and creep along any surface and adhere with

Monopodial

26

The typical upright monopodial growth of Vanda and Ascocenda orchids

great tenacity, especially in the Vandas, whose roots are utilised in the rain forest as a climbing device so plants can reach the light.

Monopodial orchids consist of only two tribes: the Sarcanthinae and the Campylocentrinae, which include Vandas, Ascocendas, Aerides, Phalaenopsis, Renantheras, Angraecums and Aerangis. The leaves are arranged in two opposite rows, the leaves of one row alternating with the other row. Leaves can be close together or far apart; most are flat and plain, although a few species produce pencil-like leaves. The inflorescence is generally a panicle – a cluster of flowers close together – as in the genera Rhyncostylis, Aerides, and Sarchochilus, although a single inflorescence occurs in Trichoglottis, Arachnis and Vandas. Branched panicles occur in mature Phalaenopsis.

Dendrochilum filiforme, *a temperate growing orchid with hundreds of tiny flowers.*

27

This basket of Masdevallias shows the sympodial orchid growth pattern

Sympodial Orchids

Most orchids are sympodial; the main axis stem (called a rhizome or pseudobulb) stops growing at the end of the season, with new growth produced in the following season. The new growth starts with leaf-like scales developing and true leaves arising between the scales; many intermediate forms sometimes occur.

A Cattleya showing the sympodial growth structure

Cattleya mossiae

The beautiful Calanthe orchids from China grow from a tuber much like Gloxinias and other bulbous plants

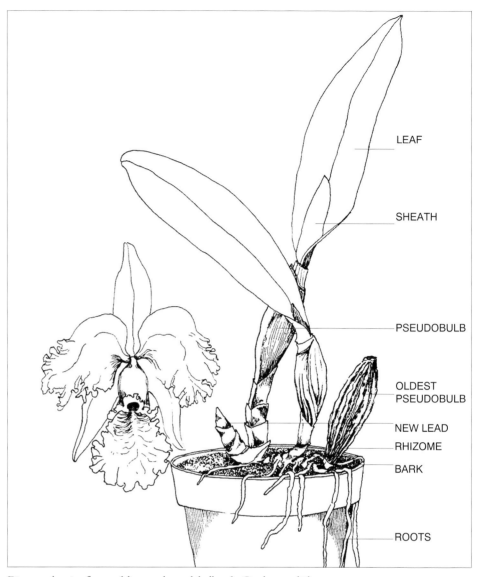

LEAF

SHEATH

PSEUDOBULB

OLDEST
PSEUDOBULB

NEW LEAD

RHIZOME

BARK

ROOTS

Diagram showing flower, foliage and pseudobulbs of a Cattleya orchid

Rhizomes and Pseudobulbs

These are primary stems from which the secondary stems develop. Rhizomes can be of various shapes and small, large, long or short, depending on the genus. In genera like Masdevallia, the rhizome is so short that it is almost unnoticeable. Pseudobulbs are storehouses of water and nutrients; if the plant cannot get water, it uses this reservoir. The pseudobulbs vary considerably in shape: *Cattleya labiata* has bulky pseudobulbs; C. *guttata* and C. *bicolor* have spindle-shaped pseudobulbs; and in the species Grammatophyllum pseudobulbs can be as big as baseballs. Laelias and Lycastes also have pronounced pseudobulbs.

In orchids with pseudobulbs and a few leaves, such as Odontoglossums, the flower spike usually develops between the first pair of true leaves. Some species produce growth of varying length and thickness. The pseudobulbs last a few years after they mature. Usually flowers are produced from new pseudobulbs, but in certain species, Epidendrums and Dendrobiums for example, flowers are borne from the same pseudobulbs or stems for several successive years.

Leaves and pseudobulbs of a typical Cattleya orchid

Flowers

Most flowers are borne in a lateral inflorescence, as with Cymbidiums, Oncidiums, Odontoglossums, Lycastes and Phaius. Variations include flowers arising from the base or side of the pseudobulb, growing on short leafless pseudobulb-like extensions near the base of the true pseudobulbs, or coming directly from the rhizome between the pseudobulbs.

Most orchids produce a terminal flower, as do the Cattleyas and most Laelias and Sobralias. On the other hand, some species, such as Lycaste and Maxillaria, display many flowers to a plant. Species like Arpophyllum bear compact spikes; the species Schomburgkia displays long flower spikes; and Phalaenopsis have long and graceful curving spikes.

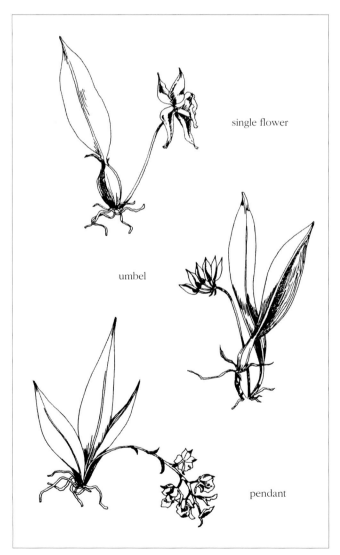

Types of orchid flower

Stenoglottis longifolia

Anguloa clowesii, *known as the Tulip orchid, has a flower of 5 to 6in.*

*Aerides odoratum –
called the Elephant
orchid because its
flowers are shaped like
tiny elephants*

*The flowers of Stelis
tollimensis are only
¼in. across – here
magnified*

*The ½in. flowers of
Koellensteinia
guatemalensis*

A specimen plant of Aerides odoratum *in the author's garden room. The plant is growing on a slab of wood; note the many aerial roots*

Roots

Roots are produced from the rhizome and are cylindrical, thickened, threadlike or branching, and usually long, as in Aerides. In epiphytic orchids, the aerial roots consist of a central axis enclosed by a covering of loose material tissue called velamen. This thin covering absorbs moisture and retains it for some time – this is the reason why some orchids can subsist on little water if necessary. Roots of most epiphytes are pendent, but in some species, such as Grammatophyllum and Catasetum, the roots grow upright. The roots search for moisture and frequently become thick and tangled, forming a basket in which falling leaves may lodge and disintegrate, providing nutrients for the orchid.

Leaves

Some leaves are fleshy and hard; others are thin and texture-like. In most deciduous orchids the thin leaves are plaited or folded. Leaves can be broad or thin, spoon- or spatula-shaped; some, as in *Brassavola digbyana*, have a somewhat fuzzy coating. Many species produce grasslike leaves; other species have club-shaped or round leaves. In most deciduous orchids the margins are solid, but some orchids display saw-toothed leaves. Because leaf variation is so tremendous, you cannot tell a specific orchid just from its leaf structure; flowers must be present for you to be absolutely sure.

The Leopard orchid Ansellia with its fine bright yellow and brown flowers

Size, Form and Mimicry

The colour and form of the orchid flower are what attract humans to the plants. Insects, on the other hand, see orchids as landing pads; they alight on the flowers and carry off the pollen, thus ensuring the propagation of the plants. The sex organs of the flowers lure the insects. Charles Darwin described this process in *On the Various Contrivances by Which British and Foreign Orchids Are Fertilised by Insects*. The book shocked the prim and proper Victorians with its openness, for the readers could not conceive of something as beautiful as an orchid flower being used for such unseemly purposes!

Orchids have three sepals and three petals plus an enlarged petal called the labellum or lip, a conspicuous part of the flower that can assume infinite shapes and forms to attract pollinators that will then help fertilise the flower. The lip may be lobed, spurred, divided, slipper-shaped, trumpet-shaped, and so on.

These complex lips operate with incredible precision. For example, in *Calopogon pulchellus*, the flower has imitation stamens, loaded with pollen that will attract insects. The lip of the Coryanthes orchids (the Bucket orchids) is shaped like a bucket to hold liquid that intoxicates insects. The insect is literally dropped into the bucket by the petals and sepals; when the insect awakens from its drunken stupor, it crawls from the flower through the lip loaded with pollen.

Some orchids mimic the insects they want to attract. *Trichoceros parviflorus* (Bee orchid) resembles a female bee and so entices the male bee. Scent also plays a role in attracting pollinators; some Cypripediums have foul odours that

Rossioglossum grande, *known as the Tiger orchid because of its striped brown and yellow flower*

Masdevallia coccinea, *the Kite orchid, does from afar resemble its common name*

invite insects. Hummingbirds pollinate Sobralias, moths pollinate Angraecums, and on and on – orchids are tough and clever and know how to seduce insects.

The wonderful world of flowers is tremendous, yet only in the Orchidaceae is there such great variation in flower size. The miniatures like Bulbophyllums and Cirrhopetalums may have flowers only one-sixteenth of an inch in size but these are clustered in many species to form a bouquet. Sobralias flaunt giant 7-9in. flowers, one to a stem. The flowers may be single or in groups of possibly fifty blossoms to a stem, as seen in the Candlestick orchid *Stenoglottis longifolia.*

Generally, the smaller the flowers the more of them there are, and while orchid flowers run the gamut from minute in size to 9in., the majority of species bear flowers 3-4in. across.

The orchid world is varied; it contains plants like Cirrhopetalum no bigger than your thumb and giant species like Grammatophyllum that grow into trees. There are others like Polyrhiza, an orchid void of leaves, and a few orchids even grow in water – Cryptanthemis and Rhizanthella.

Orchid flowers are great mimics. Some Masdevallias resemble tiny kites and many Mormodes resemble birds in flight. *Anguloa cliftonii* is called the Tulip orchid and Gongoras are called Punch-and-Judy orchids because the flowers somewhat resemble little puppets. The Spider orchid is sometimes called Arachnis or Brassia or Ansellia and the Dove orchid is *Peristeria elata.* The list goes on, but always remember that common names of plants vary from place to place, so to get the orchid you really want you must know the botanical name. Always order by botanical name, not common name.

An example of a birds-in-flight orchid, botanically known as Mormodes – deciduous orchids with fantastic flowers

Coryanthes maculata, *Bucket orchid*

Insect, funny-face – you name it. This Odontoglossum citrosmum *masquerades as many things*

Galeandra devoniana *from Venezuela and Guyana*

Oncidium luridum *growing wild in the Florida everglades*

Various orchids hugging trees – a natural way many orchids grow

～ CHAPTER 3 ～
Where Orchids Grow

Orchids grow almost worldwide, which partly explains their mystique. Collectors in the nineteenth century travelled to all parts of the globe – Royle to India, Lobb to the East Indies and Skinner to South America – to bring back the exotic plants from unknown lands, including Cattleyas from South America, Vandas from Malaysia, and Phalaenopsis from Java. Nature is generous in her bounty, but she often hides her resources in some of the remotest parts of the world, in impenetrable forests, or in insect-infested areas like Amazonia, where Margaret Mee painted orchids in their native habitat.

Geographical Distribution
Climate and temperature dictate to only a small degree where plants grow. The substantial factors are insects, birds, and certain mammals. For example, small bats pollinate Angraecum orchids; various moths help propagate other types of orchids; and birds like hummingbirds pollinate still other kinds of orchids.

Knowing the climate and temperature of the area where a particular orchid originated helps you successfully grow that orchid. Coelogynes come from cool areas such as the Himalayas, so you should try to simulate these conditions in your growing area. However, try as we may, we cannot always exactly duplicate

The lovely triangular flowers of Telipogon tessellatus, *from Peru*

the native climate of a orchid. What we can do is aim for conditions as appropriate as possible for a particular orchid; give naturally warm-growing orchids warm temperatures, and provide cooler temperatures for orchids that in the wild grow in cool climates. Remember too that most orchids prefer intermediate or temperate conditions.

New Guinea has perhaps more orchids than any other part of the world. Parts of South America – Chile, Peru, Colombia, and Ecuador – also have numerous orchids. Borneo, Mexico, Africa, England, and Florida in the United States all harbour native orchids. Oddly enough, Hawaii, which would seem to be the perfect home for orchids because of its climate, does not have any native orchids.

Cattleyas are found mainly in Venezuela, Colombia, and Ecuador, but Laelias, which grow in other countries of South America, do not thrive in those three places. Angraecums predominate in Madagascar, but a few species are also native to Japan. Phalaenopsis are from Java, but a few species originate in Cambodia, Malaysia, Borneo, and the Philippines. Phaius orchids favour a cool climate; many are from China and Japan, but others grow well in the warmth of Burma and Ceylon. Cymbidiums are native to Khasia, Nepal, and Sikkim, with some from Japan. Oncidiums are mainly from Mexico but also grow in Ecuador, Colombia, and Peru.

Most of the cultivated orchids are from tropical countries, in the region

A splendid example of Paphiopedilum praestens, *from New Guinea*

Symphyglossum sanguineum, *Peru*

Diothonea nutans, *Peru*

between the Tropic of Cancer and the Tropic of Capricorn, where rainfall is heavy (up to 100in./254cm a year) and where many countries have defined wet and dry seasons. Orchids from temperate areas also abound, but they are not as beautiful as the tropical orchids.

South America. This region of the world is home to a great number of orchid species; indeed, it was the centre of orchid collecting during the nineteenth century. The countries of this vast continent support many orchid favourites. The four basic orchid regions of South America are (1) Chile, Peru, Ecuador, and Colombia; (2) inland Argentina, Bolivia, and parts of Brazil; (3) the centre, namely, most of Brazil and Paraguay and Uruguay; and (4) the east coast of Argentina and Paraguay as well as the area around Rio de Janeiro in Brazil.

The climate varies among the four regions. The west coast varies from temperate conditions in the mountainous areas to subtropical in most of Brazil. The inner area along the west coast is somewhat cool, because of the mountains, as is the east coast of Argentina. Thus, even within the so-called temperate zones the temperatures and rainfall fluctuate to a

Masdevallia species, found in Colombia and Venezuela

Odontoglossum cordatum *from Colombia*

great degree. Most of South America has an average range of 65° to 75°F (18° to 24°C) during the day and 10°F (6°C) less at night; the rest of the country averages 52° to 64°F (11° to 18°C) during the day and 10°F (6°C) less at night. The Brazilian orchids fall between temperate and tropical (75° to 80°F/ 24° to 27°C day) temperatures (10°F/ 6°C less at night). Cattleyas and Laelias are the main South American orchids, benefiting from great air circulation near the coasts.

Epidendrum modestum *is one of the many flower forms found among Epidendrums*

Epidendrum stamfordianum – *one of more than 1,000 Epidendrum species from Mexico, Venezuela, Colombia*

The flowers of Laelia cinnabarina *sparkle like jewels in Minas Gerais, Brazil*

A Catasetum species growing on a tree in Minas Gerais, Brazil

43

Fine Zygopetalums growing in meadowland in Itambe, Brazil

Arundina graminifolia, *a tall reedy plant growing in natural habitat in Malaysia.*

A tree full of Cattleya harrisoniae *along the road to Friburgo in Brazil*

A brilliant yellow dwarf Laelia species growing among rocks

Oncidium by the road.

Lycaste Cruenta – *Mexico, Guatamala and El Salvador*

Central America and the West Indies. The west coast conglomerate of the countries of Mexico, Guatemala, El Salvador, Costa Rica, and Panama is host to many Cattleyas and Laelias. Here the temperatures are generally temperate, with nights in the 50s° to 60s°F (10° to 20°C). The east coast of Belize and Nicaragua is home to some but not an abundance of orchids. The temperatures here are about 5°F (3°C) less, day and night, than those of the west coast.

In this region of the world the rainfall also has to be considered because, like temperature, it influences the cultivation of orchids. Some years the rainfall is heavy; other years it is light. The Atlantic Coast side has both a rainy season and a dry season.

January is the coldest month, with temperatures 68° to 78°F (20° to 26°C); June and July are the warmest months, with temperatures 78° to 88°F (26° to 31°C). Guatemala, which is in a high altitude of, say, 6,000 feet (1,829m), reaches 54°F (12°C) in January and 68°F (20°C) in the warm months – favourable conditions for many orchids.

The rainy and dry seasons of Central America affect orchid growth and distribution also. The dry season is cool , and the rainy season, from June to July or August, varies in temperature because of elevation: the higher a place is in the mountains, the more rainfall the area receives. On the Atlantic Coast, the rainy and dry seasons are well defined, so orchids here require a resting period during the year. The hottest season in the West Indies is July to August, when temperatures reach 80° to 100°F (27° to 38°C).

An unidentified Maxillaria in its native habitat

Malaysia and Asia. This area includes New Guinea, Vietnam, Malaysia, Borneo, Java, Sumatra, and the Philippines. Each locale has hundreds of species, with the most in New Guinea. Paphiopedilums and Cymbidiums grow abundantly in this region, where temperatures are warm and humid with very little variation

Bulbophyllum species on 'felled' trees in Malaysia

The wonderful Bulbophyllum grandiflorum *with its elegant flowers growing on a tree at Mount Kinabalu, Malaysia*

An almost artificial-looking flower of Paphiopedilum virens *growing in shade on Mount Kinabalu, Malaysia*

throughout the year. Rainfall occurs in two distinct seasons: several months of drought followed by several months of heavy rains. This is a situation similar to that of the southern states in the United States. These regions are mainly tropical or subtropical, but some temperate zones do exist. Most orchids in this area grow in daytime temperatures of 80°F (27°C), 10°F (6°C) less at night.

Burma, China, Thailand, India, and Indonesia have many orchid species. There are vast temperature differences in these countries, greatly affected by altitude, especially in the Himalayas, where Coelogynes, and other cool-growing orchids thrive. Burma has temperate days and nights, not the hot and humid conditions most people think are common. A great many Paphiopedilums and Cymbidiums grow here.

The climate of the Malaysian peninsula and most of India is subject to only moderate changes. There are two rainy seasons: May to June and September to October. April to November usually is quite dry, similar to the conditions in northern California. The Himalayas in India, because of their varying altitudes, have a wide range of temperatures. The lowest temperatures occur in January and gradually rise, along with a big increase in rainfall until July. Rainfall can reach more than 100in. (254cm). Average monthly temperatures are 77° to 88°F (25° to 31°C). New Guinea has heavy rainfall (100 to 150in./254 to 380cm) and a rather constant temperature range of 80° to 90°F (27° to 32°C). The temperature in the Philippines varies according to elevation and location.

A showy group of Coelogyne ocellata *in the depths of debris on Mount Kinabalu, Malaysia*

The typical small flowers of Eria hyacinthoide, *from Malaysia*

49

A wonderful orchid, this Bulbophyllum sports a colourful large flower

The typical broad leaves of the genus seen on Cymbidium finlaysonianum *in Malaysia*

Laelia cinnabarina *from Brazil*

Coelogyne massangeana *foliage growing on tree in Malaysia*

Paphiopedilum argus, *with its variegated foliage, growing in the Philippines*

The wax-like blooms Paphiopedilum stonei, *from Borneo*

The fine Paphiopedilum chamberlainianum *growing among ferns*

A cascade of spring-blooming Dendrobium pierardii *adorns a tree in the Philippines*

A Macodes species growing on tree bark in Sumatra

The Jewel Orchid, Haemeria discolor, growing in its native habitat in South Borneo. It is a terrestrial shade loving orchid

A striking yellow Calanthe blooming on a mountain in Sumatra

Disa uniflora – South Africa

Africa. Africa is a vast continent of varying climatic differences because the geographical make-up covers all types of area: the Sahara and Kalahari Deserts, tropical and subtropical regions, and even mountainous sections on the east coast. Temperatures vary considerably, as does the rainfall, which ranges from 10 to 100in. (25-254cm) a year. Orchids are distributed throughout the African countries, but most are not of much horticultural interest (Africa's numerous other botanicals are what merit attention).

The equatorial zone – 12° degrees on each side of the equator – is where the epiphytic and tropical orchids thrive. Giant Angraecums cling to trees, and Eulophias grow throughout the Congo region. Beyond the equatorial zone, orchids grow irregularly.

A showy bloom of Cypripedium reginae, *an orchid from North America*

Cypripedium calceolus *one of about twelve species of this genus found in North America*

55

Xylobium squalens: *not often grown this lovely orchid thrives in coolness.*

Orchids and Climate

When orchids came into vogue in mid-nineteenth century England, the demand was such that scores of ships and dozens of orchid hunters sailed forth to find and bring back the plants that both everyday people and royalty were demanding. At first the purpose of the journeys was to find and record new flora and fauna – to open the doors to the wonderful world of natural history that England doted on.

It was a result of the trips made by the HMS *Endeavour*, HMS *Bounty* and countless other ships that orchids became the flower of the nineteenth century. Many ships sailed forth with resident artists, such as the Bauer brothers. Orchid hunters such as Roezl and Ure-Skinner risked their lives in exotic lands to capture the prized orchids for growers such as Veitch and Loddiges. It was very difficult to determine the exact area the orchids came from because each collector protected 'his' territory; thus it was thought that all orchids originated in hot, humid countries.

With the advent of the tree-type conservatory, with its ability to control temperatures to warm, temperate, and cool conditions, growers, collectors, and horticulturists became aware of how to grow the orchids. Once it was discovered that orchids came from various and dramatically different climates, and once it was known which areas specific orchids came from, the growing conditions for those orchids could be duplicated to a degree in the conservatory.

I myself discovered the importance of climate in the cultivation of orchids. In Chicago, after much experimentation, I was forced to grow only those orchids that thrived in temperate and cool temperatures. Cattleyas, Coelogynes, and Odontoglossums fared beautifully in Chicago's cold winter days of 40°F (4°C) and nights of 10° to 20°F (-12° to -7°C); I kept my solarium temperatures at 60° to 70°F (16° to 21°C) during the day, 45° to 52°F (7° to 11°C) at night.

Phalaenopsis stuartiana *in front of* Phalaenopsis schilleriana *from Indonesia*

When I moved to northern California, I found that I could grow some of the warm-, temperate-, and even cool-growing orchids. The temperatures ranged from 70° to 80°F (21° to 27°C) during the day to 45° to 55°F (7° to 13°C) at night. And when I grew orchids in the southern part of the United States, namely Florida, I found that few of my temperate-growing orchids responded; I was limited to raising warm species such as Oncidiums, Epidendrums, Encyclias, Ascocentrums, and Vandas (but of course there are more than enough warm species to suit anyone).

The lesson to be learned is that you can successfully raise orchids as long as you select the species appropriate to your growing environment, whether that is a greenhouse or a room within your home. Remembering to grow only those orchids that will thrive in your area will lead to easy growing and a gallery of collector's dreams. Thus it is important to know the background of various orchids, their geographical home and the conditions in which they grow in nature.

Dendrobium secundum *from Burma, Thailand and the Philippines. Note the wide variation in flower form in comparison with the next illustration*

Dendrobium pulchellum – *a species found in India and Burma*

Flask of seedlings ready for media potting

Cloning Orchids

The world was recently surprised by the cloning of a sheep in Scotland, but orchids have been the subject of cloning for some years. In 1961 Professor George Morel of the University of Paris meristemmed (cloned) the first orchid. He used a technique from the University of California perfected in 1946.

The apical cell (meristem) is separated from the base of a developing young growth within the plant. The shoot is then dissected and put into a liquid medium in a sterile flask. The flask must then be agitated so it is put on a revolving wheel; the constant motion inhibits the formation of a growing shoot or root so that the tiny apical meristem multiplies into many protocorms or embryo plants that are then divided. The process can be done repeatedly, thus creating a large number of plants that are replicas of the mother plant. These plants are then planted and grown as seedlings. Meristemming is a boon to conservationists because it helps prevent the extinction of certain species and preserves endangered orchids.

Cloning is best done by certified technicians in sterile laboratories. The

Typical orchid cloning laboratory

Orchid seed flasks and tissue culture at Oak Hill Gardens

Tissue culture wheel at Oak Hill Gardens with rotating orchid tissue corms

average person would have a difficult time cloning orchids because of the expense of equipment and knowledge of precision techniques. There are companies which specialise in this process and which can be hired to clone orchids for you. These companies can be found through advertisements in the various orchid journals.

The accompanying rare photos of the meristem process were supplied by Hermann Pigors of Oak Hill Gardens in Dundee, Illinois where orchids are a speciality.

Orchid clones proliferating on banana media in flask

In this exhibit lady's slipper orchids (Paphiopedilums) take the spotlight

⁓ CHAPTER 4 ⁓
Selection and Placement

Over the years, orchids have become so popular that they have attained the status of commercialised products. The orchids of most mail order dealers are reliable, and luckily most dealers are honest and knowledgeable about their plants. Orchids are now also being sold in the nursery sections of superstores whose employees usually know little about the plants. The giant stores also buy in mass, without regard for where the plants have been grown, how they have been grown, and so on. Orchids also show up at shows held in shopping malls or convention centres. It is important to familiarise yourself with what to look for in orchids, what to ask for, and how to get the most for your money. Illustrations on pages 76-68 show orchid displays at exhibitions, where the plants are all in good condition. If possible, it's a good idea to visit orchid exhibitions of displays like these to get a good idea of what a healthy plant looks like.

SELECTION
This chapter discusses in detail where plants can be purchased and covers the ramifications, good or bad, of purchasing orchids from these suppliers. This is an

A mass of varied Epidendrums which like a temperate climate

important discussion because you must start with good orchids to ensure later success in raising these plants. Inferior or weak plants will lead to frustration, whereas growing good orchids will give you years of satisfaction. And orchids can be fairly easy to cultivate; remember, in the past orchids survived three-month sea voyages to England and thrived thereafter.

Climate
Know whether your climate will accommodate the orchid you are thinking of buying. Some orchids need warmth; others prefer coolness. You would not grow Coelogynes, which are native to cool climates, in warm areas like the southern United States or the United Kingdom. Similarly, Vandas from warm countries will not thrive in the coolness of, say, the northern United States. Because there are orchids for any type of environment, you will be able to get the proper ones for your growing area; information about countries of origin and their temperatures is given in Chapter 3.

Local growers
'Local growers' here refers only to those experts selling orchids, not houseplants. A local grower is your best bet because you can see exactly what you are getting and also obtain valuable information from the grower. Such growers are listed in

Dendrobium aggregatum: *difficult to bloom but worth the patience*

telephone books or in bulletins or publications of the American Orchid Society or the *Orchid Review* of the Royal Horticultural Society in the United Kingdom.

When dealing with a local grower, inspect orchids for:

Healthy green leaves
Fresh young growth
Proper potting medium
Old flower spikes, which indicate that the orchid does bloom
Absence of insects such as aphids or mealy-bugs
Foliage free of marks or suspicious blemishes
Flowers free of twisted petals

Also pay attention to the container the orchid is in. A used or soiled container is all right. Most orchids are sold in clay pots, which are what I recommend because the clay (terracotta) is porous, so water evaporates rather than stagnating within the container. However, many people prefer to use plastic containers. If you like the look of the plastic pots, you should have no problem using them if you remember that plastic retains moisture much longer than clay.

Some local growers hold sales several times a year; they can afford to do this because they are overstocked with a particular genus. Avoid bargain table orchids and those with bare roots or in sealed plastic bags. Although bare root plants can sometimes be a good buy, it does take them longer to adjust and bloom than pre-potted orchids.

Mail Order Houses
Overall, I find mail order companies quite reliable, and usually they carry the

Brassias and Cattleyas dominate this orchid display

best orchids because their only business is to sell orchids. These suppliers want and need your business; if they want repeat customers and customers from word of mouth, they have to be honest and deal in good quality plants. Many mail order houses specialise in a particular group of orchids, say, Cymbidiums or Paphiopedilums, which is an advantage because by specialising the growers can devote all their care to these plants.

Study mail order catalogues carefully; there are so many different types and sizes of orchids offered that selection is not easy. For example, some orchids are sold as seedlings, some in small containers, and mature plants in large containers. If you can afford it, buy the mature plants. If you buy from an overseas mail order house, the shipper will take care of the necessary documentation. Travel time from overseas is usually 7-10 days by air parcel post and plants generally arrive in good shape.

Orchid Shows and Fêtes
Orchid shows are held at shopping malls, convention centres, in neighbourhood villages, banks, and so forth. Individual suppliers generally offer plants grown in your area, so the orchids have adjusted to the climate and thus have a good chance of thriving. The exhibitors provide some good buys if you know what to look for. The selection at these shows is usually quite good – a big assortment of genera – so even if you do not buy any plants, you will enjoy browsing and observing the

This is a single specimen staging with Dendrobium amethystoglossum the centrepiece

orchids. If you intend to buy some plants, plan ahead for transportation: larger orchids do not fit into cars, so if you buy several plants, you will need a van.

Flea Markets
Flea markets generally are not the most reliable places to buy orchids. Often the plants are discards the sellers want to get rid of and/or the plants are small and poorly cared for. However, occasionally you may find a mature specimen in good condition. Just shop wisely.

Various shows and fêtes are held throughout the year and categories differ. This is a mixed orchid exhibit with many genera on display

Distinguishing a good Orchid from a bad one

You do not need a keen eye or an extensive knowledge of botany to distinguish between a bad and a good orchid. All you need is the little knowledge I present here.

Plant Appearance. An orchid should look perky, not wan. Leaves should be free of blemishes, and the potting medium should be fairly new and not completely disintegrated as in fir bark potting mediums. Repotting a new orchid immediately is not recommended because the plant needs to acclimatise itself to its new surroundings, so an orchid that can stay in its original pot for a few

This Miltonia spectabilis could be a good buy; with some staking and care it could become a good specimen. Note the excellent shape of the flowers

The excellent flower form on this Masdevallia denotes a good purchase

Good flower form on this Lycaste aromatica *makes it a good buy*

Rhyncostylis gigantea. *These orchids should be uniform in growth, with good foliage. This plant does not qualify for a purchase*

months is a better buy than one that has to be repotted right away because the potting medium is too old.

Roots. Scandent roots are not a sign of a bad plant; often they indicate a plant with healthy growth and robustness. To see if roots are active, snip off a tip. Green inside means the roots are very much alive; brown inside means the roots are dead.

This Coelogyne cristata *would not be a good plant to purchase; the growth is ungainly, the leaves straggly and the plant does not have a robust quality*

This orchid room also serves as a place for dining

PLACEMENT

Orchids can be grown in many different situations. One of the most popular is indoors, directly at a window, as a houseplant (most orchids outperform other houseplants). Orchids also do well in a special area such as a garden room. In the southern part of the United States, lath houses are used often as growing areas for orchids. Decide where you want to grow your orchids, and then select the proper orchid for that location. Most orchids eventually adjust to their surroundings, but some take years. And there are easy-to-grow orchids and hard-to-grow ones. Plan carefully.

A typical Florida screened enclosure; here orchids are grown on mounted slabs on trelliswork.

In Florida a swimming pool area and screened porch accommodate dozens of hanging orchids; ample air and sun are provided

Orchids in a solarium in a Chicago, Illinois, flat. Trays on suspension poles hold plants

Window-sills

At windows orchids receive ample light, but there is a difference between light and sunlight. An east window will supply the proper sunlight, a few hours a day, which is fine for orchids. At a west window, the sun can be too hot in the summer, so orchids need protection, such as a curtain or a screen. Orchids subjected to direct sun for even a few days can burn quickly.

A south window is fine for most orchids because the exposure supplies sunlight but not too much light. And even north windows are suitable for those orchids that prefer a somewhat shady location.

Window-sills are rare in new homes, but the many new window shelving systems advertised in garden magazines are useful for displaying plants. These glass or plastic shelves come with the appropriate hardware for attaching them to windows. If you do not want the expense or the problem of installing shelf systems (and they do have their limitations), consider using what I did once: an old waist-high desk. I covered the desk with a pane of glass and set the desk next to the window; the desk easily accommodated about a dozen orchids. I put small blocks of wood under each container to lift it off the surface so air could reach plant roots from underneath.

This growing area provides plenty of light for orchids and a ceiling fan provides good air circulation

The following plants are suitable for specific exposures:

East/West windows

Aerides fieldingii
A. odoratum
Ascocentrum curvifolium
A. multiflorum
Brassavola digbyana
B. nodosa
Brassias
Dendrobium aggregatum

D. chrysotoxum
D. densiflorum
Epidendrums (Encyclias)
Laelias
Oncidium ampliatum
O. leucochilum
O. splendidum
Vandas

South windows

Cattleya aclandiae
C. amethystoglossa
C. forbesii
C. nobilior
C. trianae
C. walkeriana
Chysis bractescens

C. laevis
Lycaste aromatica
L. skinneri
Miltonias (some)
Paphiopedilums
Trichopilia suavis
T. tortilis

Orchids at a window; a tray of gravel is beneath the plants to catch excess water, and provide humidity

North windows

Coelogyne cristata
C. faccida
C. massangeana
C. ochracea
Odontoglossum grande

O. uro-skinneri
Paphiopedilums
Phalaenopsis amabilis
P. schilleriana
Sophronitis coccinea

A greenhouse situation with traps and fans – a good environment for orchids

Greenhouses, Conservatories and Garden Rooms

Whether made of glass or plastic, greenhouses and conservatories are ideal places for growing orchids. The structures are available in many sizes and designs, so you are bound to find one suitable for your taste and budget. Culture in the greenhouse or conservatory is somewhat different from that followed within the home; in these structures, orchids grow rather better and need more attention regarding watering and feeding if you want maximum results. You must consider temperature, humidity, and ventilation conditions in the conservatory or greenhouse.

A Victorian style conservatory – fine housing for orchid plants

It is best not to have an all-glass structure or the area will be too hot in the summer and too cold in the winter. Strive for home conditions, that is, average temperatures of 70° to 80°F (21° to 27°C) during the day and about 15°F (9°C) less at night. In the winter you should adjust the heat for very cold nights. In the winter, keep the structure rather cool. During very windy and cold days, provide enough heat because temperatures in the conservatory or greenhouse can drop very quickly. Sudden changes in temperature can harm orchids, so carefully manipulate windows and doors to gradually cool summer night-time temperatures. Control temperature with automatic devices like air conditioners and heaters. Remember that many orchids are not from tropical parts of the world; they are native to the temperate regions and so can take drops in temperature at night as long as the drops are not sudden.

Humidity of 30% to 60% is ideal for orchids; humidity too high can harm plants by creating a breeding ground for plant fungus and bacteria. Too much humidity and not enough circulation of air can lead to various orchid maladies. The more artificial heat you use in the winter, the more moisture in the air will be necessary. Keep the humidity quite high during very hot days; lower it at night. You do not need misters or foggers because routine watering will supply sufficient humidity.

Good ventilation provides relief from the sun, helps control disease problems, and ensures good humidity. Orchids do not object to

The author's garden room in San Rafael, California, with high ceilings and plenty of glass so adequate light reaches plants

Orchids blooming in a California garden room

Orchids are the main show in this garden room in Naples, Florida

coolness; in fact they grow better in coolness as long as ventilation is adequate. The air in the greenhouse or conservatory should be buoyant and fresh, never stagnant. Even during the winter you should provide good ventilation. Hot air rises, so have some windows or several vents at the top of the structure and open them when appropriate. If you have vents, you must have several. Put the vents on automatic timers so they will open when the temperature climbs above, say, 78°F (26°C) and close when the temperature drops below 60°F (16°C).

Except for the Vandas, orchids like diffused light, not direct and intense sunlight. If your greenhouse or conservatory has an east exposure, thus receiving only morning sun, you do not have to shade the structure. Otherwise, use movable aluminum- or wood-slatted venetian blinds or bamboo roll–ups, which are easy to install and can be opened at will.

Curtains that break the sunlight are attractive, but special window trellis is even better. You can build a trellis cheaply and install it easily; it will provide almost perfect light, creating alternate shade and light. You can also whitewash the windows, or hang shade cloth over the orchids. Nurseries sell this cloth, which comes in various size meshes (I prefer the cloth that lets in 30% or 40% of the light).

You can use gas, oil, or electric units to heat the greenhouse or conservatory. The warm-air gas-fired heater has a safety pilot and thermostatic controls; it needs an

A garden room with orchids in Marin County, California

outlet chimney for fumes. A vented heater does not need the outlet chimney. The warm-air oil-fired heater is small and furnishes sufficient heat for an average sized structure. It requires a masonry chimney or a metal smokestack above the roof. Electric heaters are automatic and have a circulating fan; heavy-duty electrical wires are necessary. (Note that a professional should install the heater and thermostats.)

Greenhouse in the Chicago Illinois area suitable for orchids at the windows

Floors constructed of concrete will absorb heat during the day, and masonry walls across from the glass or plastic wall will also absorb and store the sun's heat. Insulating glass (double glazed) is expensive but worth the cost because it can save as much as 30% heat in the growing area.

Heavy drapery will obstruct cold draughts, as will wooden shutters. Weatherstripping will keep cold air out and warm air in and can cut heat loss by about 10%. Outside the greenhouse or conservatory, landscaping with hedges and shrubs where winds, snow, and rain hit the hardest can cut the heating bill. Low-growing trees or shrubs will also cut the wind and screen out dust, pollution, and noise.

I recommend hand watering in the conservatory or greenhouse because it is the best way to observe each orchid closely. By controlling the amount of water the plants receive, you can ensure that young orchids do not rot from too much moisture.

I water early in the morning so the orchids dry out by night, to eliminate any risk of fungus and mildew.

A garden room is a glass-enclosed area, sometimes with skylights. Orchids receive enough light to thrive but not so much that they burn. Actually, the garden room is the modern version of the Victorian solarium, a place where you can sit, relax, and enjoy looking at your orchids.

Orchids in the garden room demand the same conditions as those in a greenhouse or conservatory except for shading. Since the room does not get as warm in summer as the other structures, the orchids need no shading from direct sun. If 40% of the garden room is roofed with glass, your orchids will thrive.

Interior of the author's garden room in Chicago

Hanging Devices

Hanging devices for orchids in containers are another option. These items are hung from the ceiling with appropriate hangers, usually rings of metal. Orchids suspended at a window receive maximum light and sufficient air circulation. Look for these devices at plant sections of large stores. Small wrought iron stands are attractive and reliable but expensive. You can find them listed in garden suppliers' catalogues.

~ CHAPTER 5 ~
Orchid Growing

Raising orchids is no harder than raising any houseplant. but you do need to know a few basics of containers, growing mediums, repotting, watering and humidity, feeding, insect and disease prevention, and artificial light. These may seem many factors to consider, but common sense and just the rudiments of knowledge will get you started on the road to growing healthy and happy orchids.

Containers
Certain orchids, such as the Laelias, really do much better when grown on mounts (slabs of tree fern). But most orchids will thrive in the standard terracotta flower pots sold everywhere, from nurseries to stores' garden sections. The beauty of terracotta is that it is porous, so water evaporates through it rather than stagnating within the container. If you prefer growing orchids in plastic containers, do so, but just be sure to avoid overwatering; remember, water in plastic pots will not evaporate as quickly as the moisture in the clay pots. Also, if your plastic pots retain too much moisture too long, fungus may begin to form; and because plastic containers are lightweight and tend to be top-heavy, put shards or gravel in the pots to anchor them.

Keep terracotta or plastic containers clean; scrub them with hot water before reusing them. Often an orchid will look especially stunning when placed within a decorative porcelain container such as a jardinière, cachepot or urn. Just be sure you do not plant directly in the decorative pot: plant the orchid in a terracotta pot, put a saucer under the pot, and place the pot and saucer into the porcelain container – the saucer will catch excess water. To finish off the look, add green moss to the top of the pot. Moss eventually gets waterlogged, and sometimes insects are attracted to it, so periodically replace it when you water.

Growing Mediums
Steam-dried fir or pine bark is the preferred growing medium for most orchids. It is available in fine, medium, and coarse grades and is sterile, easy to work with and inexpensive; a small bag will pot five or six orchids. I use fine-grade fir bark for Cymbidiums and Paphiopedilums, coarse-grade for Vandas and Ascocendas (these orchids need air in their root networks and the coarse-grade fir bark has more air spaces), and medium-grade for all other orchids. Other suitable growing mediums are chunks of charcoal or gravel. Be sure you buy bark that is specifically for orchids (check the package carefully); the fir bark sold as covering for paths and walks is different from orchid bark. Orchid fir bark lasts eighteen to twenty-four months, after which time it decays and becomes pulverised. It can also turn sour and stagnant and retard root growth.

Repotting
Repot most orchids every two years. To start repotting, first loosen the root ball by tapping the container rim lightly on the edge of a table or counter top. Then

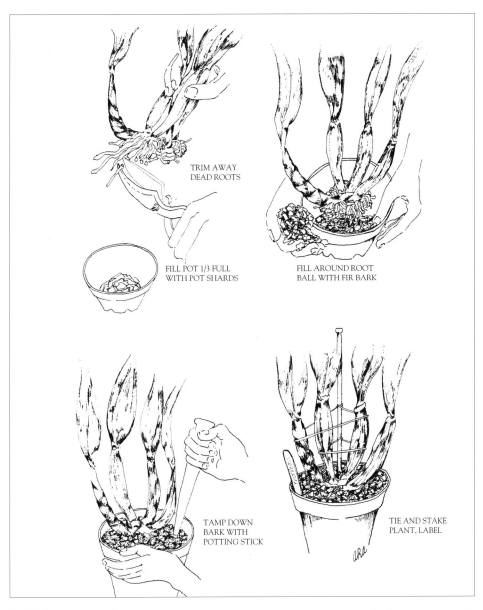

TRIM AWAY
DEAD ROOTS

FILL POT 1/3 FULL
WITH POT SHARDS

FILL AROUND ROOT
BALL WITH FIR BARK

TAMP DOWN
BARK WITH
POTTING STICK

TIE AND STAKE
PLANT, LABEL

Potting with bark

hold the crown of the orchid with one hand, the container with the other hand; gently tease the plant from the container. A few roots will break off, but this is nothing to worry about.

After you have removed the orchid from its container, gently tease away the old bark. Check the roots of the plants; cut off any that are brown or brownish black. White roots are living roots, so do not cut them. Instead, curl them around the base of the plant.

You should repot into a container the same size or 1in. (2.5cm) larger in diameter than the old one. I have found that orchids grown potbound (in pots a bit too small), especially the Miltonias and Dendrobiums, bloom better than when grown in large containers. Put shards and a layer of fresh bark into the new, clean container. Put the orchid into the new container and fill the pot with fresh bark. Tamp down the bark occasionally so the plant is securely potted, upright in the container rather than leaning. Never pot orchids loosely.

Once the orchid has been repotted, do *not* water right away. The plant should rest a day or two in a shady location to recover from the shock of repotting. After this brief rest, the plant is ready for water.

MOISTEN SPHAGNUM

TIE IN PLACE WITH STRING

POSITION PLANT

ADD OSMUNDA, TIE AGAIN AND MIST

Mounting orchids on bark

Growing Orchids on Bark or a Rack

Many orchids grow successfully when mounted on a piece of bark (small tree branch), fern slab, or a small rack such as an oven rack. To grow orchids on these mountings you must position the plants and secure the arrangement properly.

To mount a small orchid on a piece of bark or rack, wrap the roots in moist sphagnum; this material acts as a bed for the plants. Fix them in place with nylon string or galvanised wire (at hardware stores). Simply wrap the wire or string holding the plant and bedding material around the slab or branch. Then insert a small 'S'-hook into the mounting device and you can hang the mounted orchid on chains or wire from the ceiling as you would a basket container.

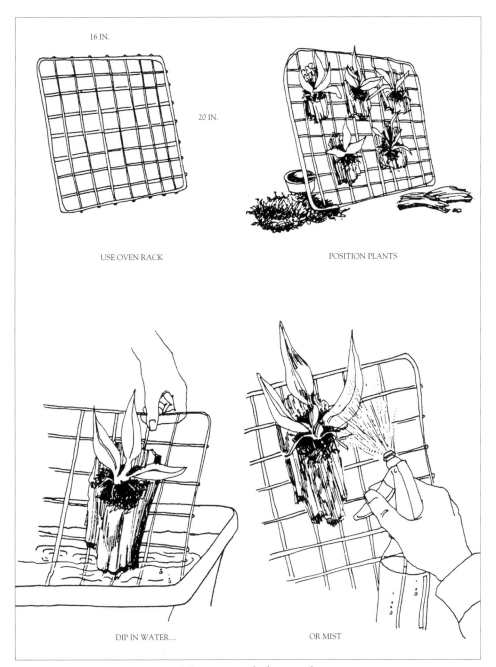

16 IN.

20 IN.

USE OVEN RACK

POSITION PLANTS

DIP IN WATER...

OR MIST

Mounting orchids on rack

To water mounted plants remove them from their place and take them to the sink. If you have a floor impervious to water (tile, brick), you can simply hose down the slab or bark. Mounted orchids rely heavily on misting so be prepared to spray them (depending on weather) at least three, four times a week).

Watering and Humidity
Tap water is fine for orchids. If your water supply contains much chloride and fluoride, let the plant water stand overnight so that the chemicals can dissipate. Water with tepid rather than cold water. It is better to water in the morning so plants can dry out by night-time (plants that are damp are susceptible to fungus). Be sure to wet all the medium when you water; newly potted orchids may take a

great deal of water. The water should flow through the entire container; catch the excess water in a saucer or water at the sink. Now water the plant again.

Small orchids in small containers will dry out faster than those in larger containers. For Cattleyas, Paphiopedilums, Phalaenopsis, Ascocendas, Vandas, Epidendrums, Oncidiums, Odontoglossums and evergreen Dendrobiums growing in terracotta containers, I follow this watering schedule:

1. Plants in small containers (to 4in./10cm): four times weekly in warm weather, two or three times a week in cold weather.
2. Plants in medium containers (to 7in./18cm): three times weekly in warm weather, twice a week in cold weather.
3. Plants in larger containers: twice weekly year-round except in the winter, then just weekly.

Deciduous orchids, such as some Dendrobiums, I let dry out severely after they bloom and do not resume watering until I see new growth. Then I water three times a week in spring and summer and once or twice a week in autumn and winter. Tapering off watering and feeding before seasonal bloom time promotes more flowers.

Misting orchid foliage can destroy certain species; water lodging in young growth causes rot, and water sprayed directly on buds can make them drop. Actually, orchids need just about 30% humidity, not the muggy atmosphere the Victorians advocated. If your plants' surroundings are exceedingly dry and you must mist, spray only the container and the growing medium, not the orchid itself.

One effective way to supply additional humidity is to elevate plants on trays containing 1in. (2.5cm) of gravel and filled with water; evaporation will add some moisture to the air. A small room humidifier of the kind that creates a fine, cool mist is good if your surroundings are overly dry. If you are growing your orchids in a greenhouse, conservatory, or garden room, and the floor is tile or brick and has drains, just hose down the growing area on very hot days – the hosing will add moisture to the air.

Feeding

Orchids do need feeding, and there are numerous plant foods on the market, in granule, liquid or systemic forms. Plant foods consist of nitrogen, phosphorus, and potash; the package or bottle of food indicates, by percentage, the amount of that element in that order. For example 30-20-10 means 30% nitrogen, 20% phosphorus, and 10% potash (the remaining 40% is filler, mainly other elements). Nitrogen promotes good leaf growth; phosphorus helps stems and flowers; and potash induces general vigour.

I use orchid foods in granule form (the granules are mixed with water), in a 30-10-10 solution for all-purpose feeding three times a month in warm weather, twice a month in winter. In addition, I use a blossom booster (10-30-20) during the seasonal bloom times (late spring for most orchids, summer for Cattleyas). I apply just enough food to moisten the bark.

The time-released fertilisers for houseplants do not work well with orchids and foliar feeding (spraying food on foliage) is not recommended because the water may accumulate in young growths. Here are the basic feeding 'rules'.

1. Ideally, feed orchids after they have been watered – never when the bark is completely dry.
2. Feed regularly and routinely.
3. Do not overfeed; too much food will either burn leaves, causing the edges to turn brown, or will kill an orchid.
4. Never apply food when the sun is shining directly on an orchid.
5. Never feed a sick orchid; feed only healthy orchids that have been watered and are in a light but not sunny location.
6. When in doubt, feed lightly rather than heavily, and feed more when plants are growing than when they are resting.
7. In cold-winter areas, stop feeding orchids in January/February.

In climates without cold winters, most orchids benefit from year-round feeding. I feed my Cattleyas, Paphiopedilums, Phalaenopsis, Ascocendas, Vandas, Epidendrums, Oncidiums, Odontoglossums, and evergreen Dendrobiums as follows:

1. For small containers, orchid food (30-10-10) twice a month from August to January; fertiliser booster (10-30-20) from February to August. 2. For large containers: orchid food once a month from August to January; fertiliser booster from February to August.

Insect and Disease Protection
Insects are not too successful in their skirmishes with orchids because the plants' leaves are so tough. Also, insects love to hide in and deposit eggs in soil, it is more difficult to do so in bark because you can see them. Any insects that go after your orchids will be from other houseplants, but at least you will be able to see any mealybugs or aphids because of orchids' growth structure.

Mealybugs look like cotton; aphids are oval-shaped; scale are brown or black and oval-shaped. Dip a cotton swab in rubbing alcohol and directly touch any of these insects with the swab (repeated applications will be necessary). Another successful weapon against these insects (and red spider mites) is a solution of half a pound of laundry soap and two gallons of water. Spray the orchids with the solution and then hose them with clear water. Several sprayings will be necessary to get rid of the insects.

Ants love to hide in the bark and build nests there. Once ants appear, mealybugs are sure to follow because ants are great herders of mealybugs, establishing colonies of them to provide protein for the young ants. If you see ants, immediately flush the bark with water and then use a good ant repellent.

Sometimes red spiders may attack orchids and turn leaves silvery and/or streaked. Use a miticide (be sure to keep such chemicals away from children and pets, and faithfully follow the directions). Also try the soap/water spray mentioned in the discussion of aphids, mealybugs, and scale.

Botanical repellents are quite safe, not persistent or harmful to the environment or humans. Effective botanical repellents are pyrethrum, rotenone, quassia, ryania, and hellebore and are available in a convenient spray forms.

Pyrethrum, from a chrysanthemum species, kills aphids on contact. Rotenone, from the derris root, fights aphids and spider mites. Quassia is a tree native to South America; an effective insect solution is made from the tree's roots and bark. Ryania

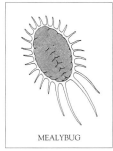

APHID

MEALYBUG

RED SPIDER MITE

Common insects

is a Latin American shrub that incapacitates beetles. Hellebore is a garden flower, of the lily family; its roots and rhizomes contain helleborin, which repels insects.

Outdoors, four insect-fighting techniques are being tested. With the sterile male technique, sterile male insects are bred and then released, overwhelming native fertile males. The premise is that if there are more sterile males than fertile ones, the fertile males have a poor chance of reaching the females before the sterile males. Possibly, females eventually will be laying infertile eggs. Experiments have been promising.

Another technique involves sex attractants that, according to the United States Department of Agriculture, offer the best possibility for developing very effective and specific ways of controlling certain insects. Among the attractants are insect lures, light and chemicals. Male insects would be lured into traps where they could be killed.

Chemical or physical repellents are effective. Wood ashes, acrylic resin (nontoxic), tar paper will deter insects. Bonemeal fights ants, as does oil of clove and camphor. Oil of citronella and ground pepper are also useful repellents.

Using high sound to control insects is a sophisticated technique not yet available for the average homeowner. Research is being conducted into using sound as an attractant, a repellent, or a way of killing insects. If a high-frequency sound heard by insects (but not humans) could be reproduced artificially, it could possibly lure insects to a trap or other device. Theoretically, the sound could be used in a wire fence to deter insects or eliminate them.

Most of the diseases that orchids may suffer from can be controlled. Botrytis (fungus disease) may attack orchids growing in insufficient light or those receiving too much moisture. Growth becomes mildewed, powdery and mushy. Chemical fungicides are available, but it is better and safer to cut away the infected parts as soon as you see them and throw them away.

Streaked or spotted areas (concentric rings) on orchid leaves indicate virus disease. Most stock used now for propagation is virus-resistant, but if you see signs of virus, remove the infected leaves at once and burn them (there is as yet no effective chemical preventative).

Leaf spot manifests itself as brown spots on leaves, caused by overly moist conditions and not enough light. Cut away the infected leaf, dust the wound with ground-up charcoal, and keep the plant slightly dry for a few days.

Brown spot is caused by splashing water that is carrying bacteria on to leaves; the resulting spots on the leaves are large and a bit watery. Cut away infected parts and dust with charcoal.

Rust appears as orange or brown raised spots, usually on the undersides of leaves. Cut away infected parts and dust with charcoal, or spray with a typical fungus remedy.

Propagation

There are several ways to increase your orchid collection. Obviously, you can buy new plants, but you can also have more plants by working with your own plants – division, offsets, backbulb growth and flower stem plantlets. These may sound really frightening procedures but are really not at all daunting. Division is simply dividing a mature plant; offset denotes taking a young plantlet from the mother plant and starting it in new media; backbulb growth and flower stem propagation are other easy methods of having more orchids for little money. Growing orchids from seed,

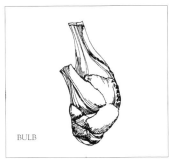

BULB

BULB AND OFFSHOOT

YOUNG PLANT

Offset division

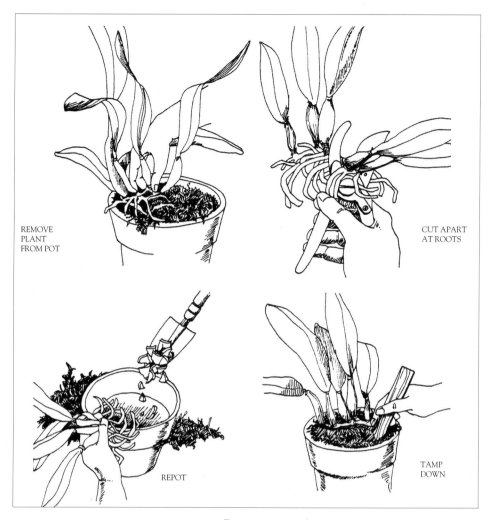

REMOVE
PLANT
FROM POT

CUT APART
AT ROOTS

REPOT

TAMP
DOWN

Division

however, is a time-consuming process – you do not see results for five years or so – and meristemmlng is best left to the experts.

To divide an orchid, take a mature plant that has at least seven bulbs (growths) and cut three of the bulbs separately. Make the cut with a sharp sterile knife. Cattleyas, bulbous Encyclias, Miltonias, Odontoglossums and Oncidiums can all be divided when mature. Spring and summer are the best times to divide plants because orchids are actively growing then and the warm weather encourages new growth. After you divide a plant put the divisions in a bright but not sunny place with good humidity. and temperature about 70°F (21°C). Do not water for the first few days; let the plant recover from the shock of surgery before starting routine watering.

Orchids such as Angraecums and Phalaenopsis frequently form offsets at the base of the plant. When the offsets have a few roots simply twist them off from the mother plant with thumb or sharp knife. Dip the offsets in a rooting hormone and put them in a separate pot. After a few days start routine watering.

If you find a single backbulb on a mature plant don't just throw it away. Pot it up; often new growth will start and you have a new plant. This method is not always successful but worth a try. Place the backbulb(s) in trays of vermiculite or perlite. Apply scant water at first and then increase watering with good humidity and warmth of 78°F (26°C).

Dendrobiums and Phalaenopsis often produce stem plantlets on their inflorescence. After roots form remove the offsets and treat them as you do regular offsets.

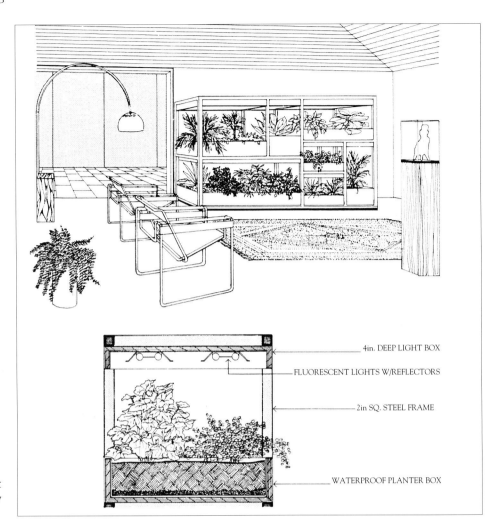

4in. DEEP LIGHT BOX

FLUORESCENT LIGHTS W/REFLECTORS

2in SQ. STEEL FRAME

WATERPROOF PLANTER BOX

Freestanding metal unit showing the perspective view and a section

Artificial Light

The use of plant lamps to stimulate growth in plants is sophisticated today, unlike several years ago when I used standard fluorescent tubes for some orchids at home. Today these tubes come in various 'light' combinations and wattages – in grow-type lamps and Halide lamps and in sodium-type lamps – all designed to enhance plant growth. Trade names differ throughout the world. Suitable canopies and reflectors for lamps vary as well and are available under trade names at suppliers.

Orchids can be grown under artificial light in several areas round the home: in a room divider, a wall niche planter, in a freestanding unit or along a countertops. Like a rainbow, the visible spectrum is composed of colours ranging from red to violet. It is the blue, red and far-red light waves plants need to grow. Blue light enables plants to manufacture carbohydrates. Red light controls the assimilation of these and affects photoperiodism – a plants' response to the relative lengths of day and night. Far-red is one of the colours that influences plant growth. It has an elongated effect on plant stems and generally increases leaf size. It is quite possible that yellow light also plays some role in plant growth.

Light intensity and duration work together with night temperatures to influence how plants bloom and grow. Each orchid is apparently individual in its needs.

Standard fluorescent lamps are available in cool white, warm white, daylight and natural white and they emit red and blue waves of light. Cool white are the tubes I used for my light experiments. There are also special plant tubes: Gro-Lux

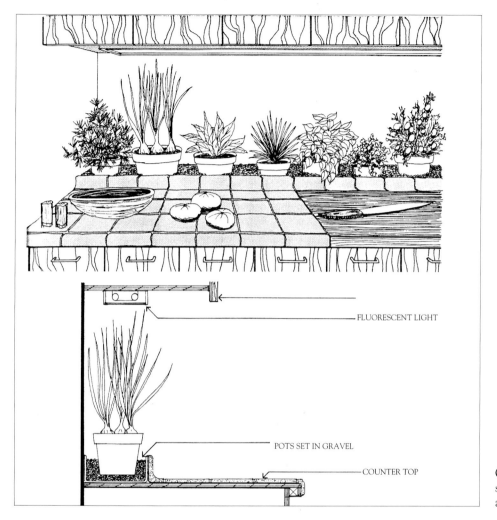

FLUORESCENT LIGHT

POTS SET IN GRAVEL

COUNTER TOP

Countertop Plant Trough
showing the perspective view
and the cross section

and Sylvania's Wide-spectrum lamps. These lamps (tubes) come in various lengths. Halide lamps are said to have a 50% increase in the overall spectrum; sodium lamps are sometimes used in combination with Halide types. I can only vouch for the standard fluorescent lamps I used – they did increase growth in some orchids but, because of the complexities of long-day, short-day and day-neutral orchids, it became tedious to keep proper times that lamps should be on (and times change with the changing of the seasons). I was successful to some degree to get Paphiopedilums and some Cattleyas to bloom and some of the Odontoglossums also responded but, in total, my one year experiment with artificial light was not completely satisfactory. However, my failure might be your success.

In addition to reflectors there are various artificial light hardware units available. Table models can accommodate about twenty-four plants and floor models can hold many more orchids.

In general I used 20 watts of artificial light per square foot of growing area and kept the tops of the plants 8-10ins. from the lamps. I bought a commercial reflector stand setup from an orchid supplier. Temperature and humidity and careful watering of plants must be supplied when using artificial light – cultivation is different from growing plants at a window and experimentation is the keyword to success when employing artificial light.

Investigate light systems carefully and fully; there are many different kinds and types to choose from.

Catasetum by W.H. Fitch

Laelia purpurata

Disa grandiflora *from* Cool Orchids & How to Grow Them *by F.W. Burbridge, London 1874*

∼ CHAPTER 6 ∼
Orchids Illustrated

A perusal of the many wonderful florilegia of the 19th century reveals a dominance of orchids. Within Robert Warner's *Orchid Album: Select Orchidaceous Plants (1862-91)*; and James Bateman's *Orchidaceae of Mexico and Guatemala* (1837-43 and probably the biggest book ever published) are thousands of illustrations of orchids. Publications also displayed beautiful drawings of these favoured plants. Curtis's *Botanical Magazine* (first published 1787 and still being published as *Curtis's Botanical Magazine incorporating the Kew Magazine*) and numerous other periodicals such as Loddiges' *Botanical Cabinet* (1818-33), Joseph Paxton's *Paxtons (Magazine of Botany)* (1834-49), Louis van Houtte's *Flore des Serres et des Jardins de L'Europe* (1845-1883), and others, included the works of such distinguished botanical illustrators as Sydenham Edwards, Mrs. Augusta Withers, P.-J. Redouté, J. Andrews and others.

Because of the various forms of the orchid flowers – from the tiny elephant-shaped flower of Rhyncostylis to the unusual flowers of the Swan orchid Cycnoches and the dazzling Dendrobiums with flowers that look like a bunch of grapes on a stem – the orchid was a perfect subject for artists to depict on paper.

Odontoglossum by W.H. Fitch

Stanhopea, one of the few orchids that blooms from the bottom of the plant.

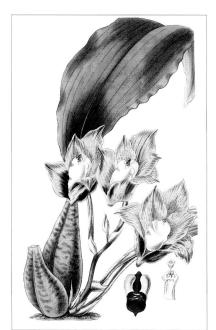

Zygopetalum from Curtis's Botanical Magazine, 1832

Catasetum from Lucien Linden's Lindenia

Cattleya harrisoniana from Lucien Linden's Lindenia

Oncidium forbesii

Today the hand-coloured drawings (stippled or aquatinted) are valuable and sought after by collectors, and their true beauty is displayed at many museums throughout the world. In their major work *The Art of Botanical Illustration* (Antique Collectors' Club 1994), Wilfrid Blunt and William Stearn write these apposite words: 'No other family [of plants] has been so despoiled by collectors and so honoured in botanical art as the Orchidaceae.'

Books on how to grow orchids became popular and Lewis Castle's *Orchids, Their Structure, History and Culture* (London 1887), *Sander's Orchid Guide*

Cattleya labiata from Loddiges' Botanical Cabinet, *London 1818-1833*

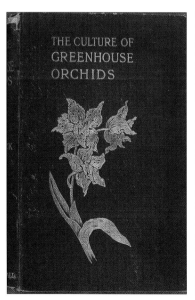

Cover of Boyle's The Culture of Greenhouse Orchids, *1902*

Cypripedium luteum *from Rafinesque C.S. Medical Flora, Philadelphia, 1828*

Engraving from Castle's Orchids, Their Structure, History and Culture, *London 1887*

Cattleya lawrenciana *by John Nugent Fitch*

(originally published in 1875 in Antwerp), and *The Orchid-Growers' Manual* by B.S. Williams (London 1894 edition) were all successful works that were printed in many editions to educate the public on growing the majestic orchid. These were handsome books with fine engravings and the cultural information contained within the covers is very close to the advice still given today on growing orchids.

A word of warning, orchid taxonomy has changed in one hundred years so names of orchids in some of these publications may now be different in some cases.

The illustrations in this chapter are just a small selection. They reflect the enormous interest in orchids, an interest which was also reflected in 19th century fabrics, wallpaper, jewellery and embroidery.

Cypripedium insigne

∽ CHAPTER 7 ∽
Gallery of Orchids

This gallery contains descriptions of more than three hundred orchids. Temperatures are given in Fahrenheit (F) with Centigrade (C) noted in parentheses. The night-time temperature should be 7° to 10°(F) (about 5°C) lower than daytime temperatures.

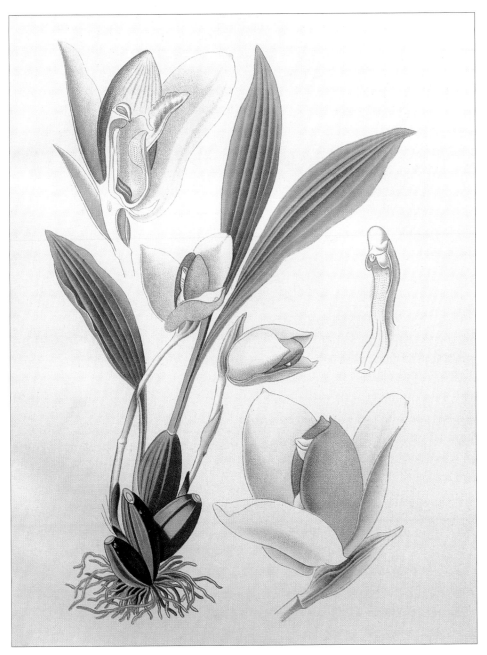

Lycaste skinneri

Cool	45° to 58°F (7° to 14°C)
Temperate	58° to 80°F (14° to 27°C)
Warm	80° to 90°F (27° to 32°C)

The (approximate) date is when the orchid genus was first described in a publication or first introduced.

Measurements are given in inches (in.), with centimetres (cm) listed in parentheses and rounded up or down.

Species names are those commonly used now. (Taxonomists change names as classification progresses and thus some species names listed here may have changed by the time of publication.) Any common names are included when applicable.

Acampe pachyglossa

Acampe   Temperate   1853

Acampe does well in temperate home or greenhouse conditions when grown in large-grade fir or pine bark. The small and waxy flowers are usually yellow, accented with red spots or red shading, and last about one month. This genus of epiphytic orchids from India and Asia includes fifteen known species allied with Vandas but needing different culture.

A. pachyglossa likes a sunny location and lots of water but is not fussy about temperature. The small yellow flowers are striped red, twenty to a cluster; plants in the right conditions will bloom twice during the warm months.

A. papillosa is similar.

Hint: If you have trouble getting Acampe to bloom, lower the night-time temperature a few degrees.

Acanthophippium montinianum

Acanthophippium (cup of Gold orchid)   Warm 1825

These terrestrial orchids should be grown in a compost of equal parts of fir bark and soil, in a warm location that receives scattered sunshine. Acanthophippiums like heavy watering except before and after flowering. The large cup-shaped red and yellow flowers are on display in June and last about a month.

A. montinianum blooms with 3in. (8cm) yellow and red waxy flowers that are a beautiful tulip shape.

Hint: These orchids are extremely difficult to get to bloom. Try growing them in a straight houseplant medium.

Acineta   Cool/Temperate   1843

This genus of twelve species includes epiphytic or sometimes terrestrial orchids from southern Mexico to Ecuador and Venezuela. The broad leaves are 24-30in. (61-76cm) long; the dramatic flowers, borne on pendent scapes, are usually yellow or white, with red spots. Acinetas prefer cool temperatures and grow well in the home or greenhouse, in fir bark with heavy watering except after flowering, when they should be rested for three weeks. Give these orchids a shady and moist location that gets warmth during the day and is cool at night. Grow this orchid in a slatted basket to allow the pendant flowers scape to bud and bloom.

A. chrysantha (densa) blooms with waxy and fragrant cup-shaped flowers in the spring.

A. superba has pale yellow flowers spotted with brownish-purple or red; the blooms are 3in. (8cm) in diameter.

Hints: Acinetas are true collector's orchids. They are usually easy to bring to bloom. Do not fuss over these orchids.

Acineta superba

Aerangis fastuosa

fragrant flowers.

A. fastuosa produces handsome small flowers, many to a plant.

A. kirkii has pure white aromatic flowers and 5in. (13cm) long leaves.

A. kotschyana is remarkable for its star-shaped white flowers and the long twisting tail of the inflorescence.

A. rhodosticta bears many spectacular pure white flowers that have a red centre.

Aerides   Temperate   1790

Here is a delightful genus of inexpensive miniature and large orchids; the sixty epiphytic species are native to tropical Asia. Pot Aerides in fir or pine bark; water plants heavily while they are growing, but let them dry out for about a month after they flower (keep them barely moist). Aerides should always be in a sunny location, and they prefer brightness and good air circulation. However, if necessary they will tolerate coolness (56°F/13°C at night).

A. crassifolium has many exquisite fragrant purple flowers in June. The leaves are 6-9in. (15-23cm) long.

A. japonicum is the smallest species, with leaves only 3-4in. (8-10cm) long. The branched flower spikes bear fragrant white blooms marked with red.

A. odoratum produces pleasantly scented creamy rose flowers with some white, spotted purple in the summer.

Hint: Aerides can be difficult to bring to bloom. These orchids need a great deal of light.

Aerangis   Temperate   1865

The genus Aerangis is comprised of seventy epiphytic species from the Malagasy Republic and tropical Africa. These small and expensive orchids, relatives of the Angraecums, produce white flowers in the winter and do not need too much attention. In nature the orchids grow in warm temperatures with lots of moisture and sunlight, but they adjust well to cool nights of, say, 54°F (12°C). Grow Aerangis in fine-grade fir or pine bark and water them year round.

A. biloba has 6in. (15cm) leaves and charming 1in. (3cm)

Angraecum (Comet orchid) Cool/Temperate   1804

Angraecums are large, miniature or dwarf, with fan-shaped growth. The genus encompasses 200 species, mostly epiphytic, distributed throughout Africa (a few are native to Sri Lanka). The white, star-shaped flowers bloom for more than a month. Grow Angraecums in coarse-grade fir or pine bark in the home or greenhouse; give them lots of

Aerangis rhodosticta

Aerangis biloba

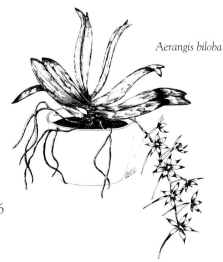

Aerides odoratum

Angraecum compactum

bright light (but out of direct sun). They can tolerate minimum night-time temperatures of 60°F (16°C) and need good air circulation and a moist atmosphere. Repot plants only when necessary.

A. compactum is a delightful miniature, only 5in. (13cm) high, with 2in. (5cm) aromatic and stunning white flowers.

A. eburneum has as many as a dozen greenish white flowers to a stem. This Angraecum grows about 36in. (91cm) high. A healthy plant will bear several stems at once and produce very fragrant flowers.

A. eichlerianum is a tall, rambling plant with light green leaves and greenish white flowers tinted brown. The flowers, about 2in. (5cm) long, are borne singly or in pairs.

A. falcatum (Neofinetia falcata), another miniature, grows 6in. (15cm) high and bears wonderfully scented 1in. (3cm) white flowers.

A. leonis, a dwarf, bears fine white flowers with long spurs.

A. sesquipedale has fleshy and fragrant 7in. (18cm) flowers that are waxy white with greenish-white spurs. Most growers classify it as warm-growing, but I have grown it successfully in night-time temperatures of 56°F (13°C); it bloomed in February.

A. veitchii, a hybrid, is very floriferous, producing waxy and white star-shaped flowers in the winter.

Angraecum leonis

Anguloa (Tulip or Goblet orchid)
Cool/Temperate   1794

The twelve species of this genus are native to the high
regions of Colombia, Venezuela, Ecuador and Peru. These
terrestrial or epiphytic orchids are close relatives of the
Lycastes. Several scapes produce one spectacularly large
flower per scape. The colour of the flowers is variable but is
generally yellow with a waxy texture. The fragrance is
delightful.

While they are growing, Anguloas need some warmth,
but when growth matures, plants prefer cool to temperate
conditions. Grow these orchids in the home or a cool
greenhouse, in a well-ventilated spot with no excessive
dampness but some afternoon sun. Flood plants with water
as they are growing, but when the pseudobulbs mature,
give the orchids a three-week rest. Resume watering when
flowers appear (usually in the summer); after plants bloom,
move them to a cooler spot (about 58°F/14°C). During the
winter, keep them barely moist, to avoid rot. Keep
moisture from the centre of the young growth.
A. *cliftonii* has large, golden-yellow flowers marked with
purple-brown. It needs careful attention to resting time.
A. *clowesii* grows about 30in. (76cm) high and bears showy 3in.
(8cm) yellow, sometimes almost orange, waxy flowers in May.
A. *ruckeri* bears large cup-shaped orange-red flowers.
A. *uniflora* produces flowers that are smaller than those of
other species. The waxy white or cream-white flowers are
cup-shaped and flushed with pink.
Hint: Anguloas like to be cool.

Ansellia (Leopard orchid)   Warm   1844

This genus from Africa does best when grown in
greenhouse rather than home conditions. It can last years
in the same pot and includes some large species, so you
need sufficient space. It is usually grown warm, but
Ansellia can adjust to coolness. A mature Ansellia carries
about fifty stunning 2in. (5cm) yellow and brownish red
flowers (but even young plants bloom, with a smaller

Anguloa ruckeri

Anguloa clowesii

Ansellia africana

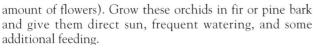
Arachnis flos aeri

Arpophyllum spicatum

amount of flowers). Grow these orchids in fir or pine bark and give them direct sun, frequent watering, and some additional feeding.

A. *africana (gigantea)* is very amenable and tolerates fluctuating temperatures and neglect. Small flowers are yellow barred with brown; the larger 3in. (8cm) flowers of other Ansellias are yellow lined with brilliant red.

Hint: Ansellias are generally easy to grow.

Arachnis   **Warm**   **1825**

This genus of fifteen species is closely allied to the Vanda genus. The orchids are native from the Himalayas to New Guinea to the Solomon Islands. Species are tall- or short-stemmed; all species are free-flowering, some with as many as thirty multicoloured blossoms. Arachnis will grow in pots, but they really thrive in raised beds of garden loam, full sun, heavy watering, and some fertilising.

A. *clarkei* is about 72in. (183cm) high. The yellow sepals of the flowers are yellow; petals are barred chestnut-brown.

A. *flos-aeris (moschifera)* grows to 168in. (427cm) in height and has leathery leaves that are about 8in. (20cm) long.

The faintly scented flowers, greenish-white or yellow blotched with chocolate-red, bloom for a long time.

Hint: Not outstanding.

Arpophyllum   **Warm**   **1825**

This group of orchids from Mexico and Central America has only a few species. The plants generally are terrestrial and produce an unusual flower scape resembling a hyacinth: a spike loaded with densely spaced pink flowers. My specimens did very well in a temperate situation, but they thrived for only a few years and then gave up completely. My failure may lead to your success: I believe the plants needed more sun and a rich soil rather than the medium I grew them in. I also think they needed more heat than I was able to provide, perhaps a minimum of 64°F (18°C) at night.

A. *spicatum* was the species I grew, but the name may not be correct. I have never been able to track down its authenticity.

Hint: Watering may be the factor contributing to successful growing of this orchid.

Arundina   **Warm**   **1825**

From southern China and the Himalayas, this genus has one species available: A. *graminifolia*, which thrives better in the ground than in a container. Grow Arundina in rich garden loam and give it lots of water, warmth, humidity, and sunlight.

A. *graminifolia* produces wonderfully fragrant flowers that are 2-3in. (5-8cm) in diameter. The sepals and petals are light rose; the lip is rose. The front lobe is a deep purple, and the throat is white, lined with orange. A mature A. *graminifolia* will bloom for several months in the summer.

Hint: The large and dramatic flowers last only a few days.

Ascocentrum   **Warm/Temperate**   **1913**

This genus of epiphytic orchid has nine species, native to India, Burma and Malaysia. Sometimes called Saccolabium, the orchids bear spectacularly coloured flowers: orange, red, rose-purple. Spikes may have as many

Ascocentrum ampullaceum

as thirty flowers on them, and the flowers last for several weeks. Grow Ascocentrums in fir bark. Keep plants very moist, but never let the bark get soggy. Plants like bright light, 30% to 50% humidity.

A. *ampullaceum* bears clusters of bright rose-carmine flowers with a spurred yellow lip in the autumn. It is an excellent house-plant. Water it two or three times a week if the weather is sunny, less on cloudy days.

A. *curvifolium* blooms in the autumn with cinnabar-red 1in. (3cm) flowers. It needs its growing medium evenly moist and does not tolerate fluctuations in temperature, so keep it in one spot.

A. *micranthum* is summer-flowering, with clusters of ½in. (2cm) white flowers marked with lavender and looking like small winged insects. It needs good humidity and can tolerate coolness

Arundina graminifolia

Ascocentrum curvifolium

A. *miniatum* is small and in the autumn produces orange flowers. It needs even moisture.

A. *pumilum* has ½in. (2cm) flowers in the winter. Sepals and petals are lavender to pink, with a green inner throat and a deep lavender dot above the throat. It needs good air circulation and spraying every few days.

Hint: Water evenly year-round.

Ascocentrum miniatum

*Bifrenaria
harrisoniae*

Bifrenaria   Temperate   1833
These epiphytic orchids, mainly native to Brazil, include
about twelve species. Seldom seen in cultivation,
Bifrenarias are handsome, producing large and showy
flowers. *B. harrisoniae* and *B. tyrianthina* are the only two
species commercially available (they are similar in habit).
Because Bifrenarias grow compactly, these orchids are
perfect for areas of limited space. The pseudobulbs are 1-
3in. (3-8cm) long; the flowers appear in the spring.
  Grow Bifrenarias cool (55°-58° F/12° -14°C at night in
winter), with two to three hours of filtered, not direct, sun
during the day. Plant the orchids in medium-grade fir or
pine bark in 5 or 6in. (13 or 15cm) slotted orchid clay

Barkeria skinneri

Barkeria   Temperate   1838
These handsome orchids, in cultivation since 1838, are
named after George Barker of England, an avid orchid
grower. The genus has moved back and forth between
Epidendrum and Encyclia; now it is Barkeria. The orchids
are indigenous to Mexico and the West Indies.
  Barkerias are relatively easy to grow in a somewhat cool
location at night (58°F/14°C), and they need some dappled
sunlight. They prosper in fir bark or lava rock; give them
the excellent drainage they demand. Barkerias have grassy
leaves and handsome rose-lilac flowers that are large for the
size of the plants.
B. lindleyana, the most frequently seen species, grows to
about 16in. (41cm) and has shown lilac flowers.
B. skinneri is similar to *B. lindleyana* but has a somewhat
smaller flower.

Bifrenaria tyrianthina

Bletia striata

pots; repot only every second year.

After the plants flower, give Bifrenarias a three to five week rest, but do not let the pseudobulbs get so dry that they shrivel. Repot now if necessary. Once new growth appears, resume watering, increasing the amount as growth develops. Keep the fir or pine bark just evenly moist during the growing season.

B. harrisoniae produces one or two large (3in./8cm across) flowers. The sepals and petals are cream-white to yellow and big and fleshy. The lip is reddish- purple and slightly haired and marked with purple veins, streaked inside with red. Flowers last about three weeks.

B. tyrianthina is somewhat larger, with large reddish-purple flowers, the lip coloured with deeper veins.

Hint: Cool night-time temperatures will bring on flowers.

Bletia   Cool/Temperate   1731
Native to tropical America, Brazil and Peru, this genus of more than fifty species is mainly terrestrial. The five main species available produce pretty pink to rose flowers. The pseudobulbs are round and rather flat; foliage is deciduous or nearly deciduous and 24-48in. (61-122cm) tall. Flower scapes can reach 36in. (91cm) in length, erect or arching under their own weight. The flowers are short-lived but are produced one after another, so a plant can be in bloom for as long as nine weeks. Cut flowers also last a long time in water.

In the winter give Bletias as much sun as possible, but in the summer grow them at a west rather than a south or east window. These terrestrials need a compost of leaf mould, sand and fibrous loam (plants also do well in commercial African violet soil). Be sure containers have good drainage. Repot Bletias only when absolutely necessary (but do add fresh compost to the top of the growing medium now and then).

Bletias need lots of water while growing, but when leaves start falling decrease watering a bit. After the orchids flower, give them a bone-dry rest in a slightly shaded location until signs of new growth appear, usually in six to eight weeks. Then resume watering, moderately at first and increasing as growth develops.

Bletias prefer slightly cool night-time temperatures and dislike a hot or stuffy atmosphere – good air circulation is a must. If you have trouble growing Bletias, give them more shade and cooler temperatures; plants will do quite well but may not flower as much as they would in ideal conditions.

B. gracilis displays striking pale purple or purple-rose flowers 1-2in. (3-5cm) in diameter. The green lip is veined dark red and purple.

B. purpurea produces six to twelve pink or rose flowers about 1½in. (4cm) in diameter. The flowers do not fully open; the petals form an open hood over the lip. *B. purpurea* is easier to grow than other Bletias.

B. shepherdii blooms in the winter; the pink or rose blooms are 2½in. (6cm) in diameter.

B. sherratiana catenulata is the prettiest Bletia but the hardest to find. The small flowers are textured and rosy-red, with a dark purple lip lined with yellow.

B. striata has small rose-pink flowers, many to a stem.

Bletilla lindeyana

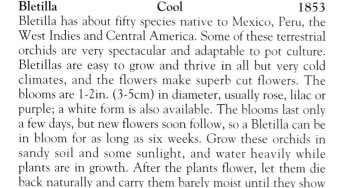

Bletia striata

Bletilla   **Cool**   **1853**

Bletilla has about fifty species native to Mexico, Peru, the West Indies and Central America. Some of these terrestrial orchids are very spectacular and adaptable to pot culture. Bletillas are easy to grow and thrive in all but very cold climates, and the flowers make superb cut flowers. The blooms are 1-2in. (3-5cm) in diameter, usually rose, lilac or purple; a white form is also available. The blooms last only a few days, but new flowers soon follow, so a Bletilla can be in bloom for as long as six weeks. Grow these orchids in sandy soil and some sunlight, and water heavily while plants are in growth. After the plants flower, let them die back naturally and carry them barely moist until they show signs of new growth.

B. lindeyana has small violet flowers, many to a stem.

B. purpurea usually has six to twelve pink or rose 1½in. (4cm) diameter flowers that do not open fully. This Bletilla is easy to grow.

B. skinneri has foliage about 36in. (91cm) tall and 1in. (3cm) rose-purple flowers.

Bollea   **Cool/Temperate**   **1852**

Overlooked, the genus Bollea offers fine plants for cultivation. From Central and South America, notably Colombia, this group once was included with Zygopetalum but more resembles Pescatorea. The large flowers, to 4in. (10cm) in diameter, are a beautiful violet marked white at the tips of the petals. The growth is clump-like, forming a fan; in the summer, flowers are borne singly from the base of the plant.

Bollea ecuadoriana

At one time these orchids were grown in warmth, but they really prefer coolness. Plants must be watered carefully because excess water lodged in the leaf axils can cause rot, so keep the fir bark evenly moist year-round.

B. coelestis is somewhat dwarfish; the foliage is quite attractive and the flowers are large.

B. ecuadoriana displays beautiful violet-red flowers.
B. violacea has especially handsome wavy-edged petals and intense violet-blue colouring blotched white.

Hint: The flowers are excellent; be sure to water plants carefully.

Bollea violacea

Brassavola glauca alba

Brassavola   **Warm**   **1813**

Distributed mainly throughout Central America, Brassavolas are epiphytic orchids producing scented white or greenish white flowers that last two to three weeks. Some members have been reclassified into the genus Rhyncholaelia, but I use the old name. Most species have stem-like pseudobulbs topped by one cactus-like leaf. Blooming is generally in the summer, but some varieties may bloom in the autumn.

Brassavolas like lots of sun; they will adjust to varying temperatures, but they prefer temperate conditions. Grow these orchids in medium-grade fir or pine bark. They resent repotting, so, when necessary, dig out decayed bark with a stick and replace it with fresh bark around the root ball. Keep the growing medium evenly moist year-round, but in the winter give plants less water than during the rest of the year.

The leaves of the Brassavolas are so tough that insects rarely bother them. If your Brassavolas do not bloom, try growing them in a cooler temperature, say 56°F (13°C) at night, to encourage flower buds.

B. cucullata is small, but its flower is about 2in. (5cm) in diameter and spotted with purple. This easy-to-grow Brassavola makes a perfect house-plant.

B. digbyana (Rhyncholaelia digbyana), one of the most beautiful orchids grown, produces one lone flower that is 6in. (15cm) across, pale green with a handsomely fringed white lip. It is often used for hybridising.

B. glauca alba produces a waxy flower that has a heady scent.

B. nodosa (Lady of the Night) is famous for its wonderful evening scent. The pale green flowers have narrow sepals and petals and a scalloped lip.

Hint: Dry out the plants somewhat in the early spring to force flowers.

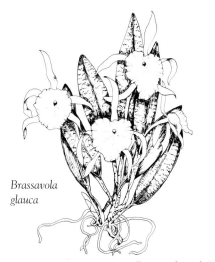

Brassavola glauca

Brassavola nodosa

Brassia gireoudiana

Brassia   **Temperate**   **1813**

The epiphytic Spider orchids, native to Brazil, Peru, Mexico, Costa Rica and Guatemala, are favourites because they hybridise very well with Odontoglossums and Oncidiums. The pseudobulbs are plump; the leaves are dark green. The flowers are white or pale yellow dotted with brown and appear in the late spring through the summer.

Brassias like a buoyant atmosphere (they will not do well in stagnant air), and good humidity (about 40%). If your plants do not do well in one spot, move them until you find a spot they like: Brassias are sensitive to location.

Give plants lots of water while they are growing, but slightly dry them out in the autumn to discourage foliage growth and help start flower spikes. Resume watering when spikes appear. During the winter, decrease watering, but do not let plants get bone dry. If your home is very dry, mist the container or potting mixture in the early morning so the pot or mixture is dry by night-time. Do not overfeed Brassias; 30-20-10 twice a month in the spring and summer is fine, with very little or no food during the winter.

Grow Brassias in medium-grade fir or pine bark, with some charcoal chips added. Let the plants crowd their containers. Repot every second year; these plants really resent having their roots disturbed. Use only clay containers so moisture can evaporate quickly; plastic retains moisture too long, which means the growing medium gets too wet and the roots become injured.

B. caudata grows to 20in. (51cm) in height and displays light green flowers that sometimes are tinted yellow and spotted with dark brown on the lip.

B. gireoudiana has flower scapes that may grow as long as 24in. (61cm). The flowers are yellow or greenish-yellow with a few blotches of dark brown. This is the most fragrant of the Brassias; it blooms irregularly.

B. longissima bears 7in. (18cm) diameter (or larger) eggshell-yellow flowers spotted reddish brown. The pseudobulbs are large.

B. maculata grows to 30in. (76cm). The plant bears six to twelve flowers with 4in. (10cm) sepals. The petals are shorter and greenish-yellow spotted with brown. The spreading white lip is marked with brown or purple.

B. verrucunda has long sepals and white petals marked greenish-brown. This Brassia grows to 30in. (76cm).

Hint: Give plants good air movement.

Brassia maculata

Bulbophyllum (Cirrhopetalum) medusae

Bulbophyllum　　　　　**Warm**　　　　　**1822**
This genus has more than 2,000 species native to the tropics and subtropics. These epiphytic orchids produce small and intricate flowers that bloom in every colour but blue and black (greenish-brown is the most common colour). Grow these 6in. (15cm) plants in warm conditions, and keep them moist year-round. Bulbophyllums do best grown on fir bark slabs exposed to the sun.
B. barbigerum produces an intricate flower with purple-brown hairs.
B. grandiflorum produces an elegant flower, tawny-beige.
B. lemniscatoides has dark purple flowers; the sepals have white hairs and a white and spotted red trailing ribbon appendage.
B. lobbii, a small plant produces large hooded flowers of brownish-yellow; unusual.
B. medusae (Cirrhopetalum medusae) displays straw-coloured flowers.
B. morphoglorum produces several hundred small blooms that are yellowish-brown, spotted brown, making this orchid most unusual.
B. rothschildianum (see *Cirrhopetalum longissimum*)
Hint: Be careful about watering: Bulbophyllums must grow in evenly moist, never wet, conditions.

Calanthe　　　　　**Warm/Temperate**　　　　　**182**
These are truly collectors' orchids, not to be missed by any orchid enthusiast. Calanthes are native to Asia and China. The genus is divided into two types: the large-bulb deciduous types such as *C. labrosa*, *C. rosea* and *C. vestita*, and the pseudobulbless evergreen types such as *C. biloba*, *C. masuca*, and *C. veratrifolia*.

The deciduous Calanthes bear three or four paper-thin leaves about 20in. (51cm) high. The flower spike, produced after the leaves shed, carries many small white or pink blooms during the Christmas season. The flowers last five to seven weeks. This type of Calanthe needs filtered sunlight when growth starts and full sun once leaves have expanded. Pot these terrestrials in March or at signs of new growth in a mixture of loam, leaf mould and sphagnum.

Bulbophyllum morphoglorum

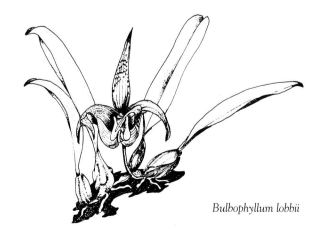

Bulbophyllum lobbii

Calanthe rosea

Water the deciduous Calanthes carefully until foliage opens; then increase waterings and keep plants evenly moist throughout the summer. When the foliage begins shedding (towards the autumn), considerably reduce waterings, to encourage flower spikes. When the spikes are 2-3in. (5-8cm) long, apply moisture to the medium until buds are plump; do not wet the spike. When the first flowers open, stop watering completely. After plants flower, you can cut off the spike, take the plant from its pot, and store the bulbs in a brown bag at 60°F (16°C). The following spring, separate the bulbs and pot them. These plants are superb as table decoration or as cut flowers.

C. labrosa has small rose-purple flowers whose lips are dotted with purple.

C. rosea bears small pale pink, almost white, flowers.

C. vestita bears white or pink flowers 1-2in. (3-5cm) in diameter.

The evergreen Calanthes are excellent houseplants; they look like Chinese evergreens, with tall, folded, dark green leaves growing in a compact bunch. The purple- or rose-coloured flowers, which appear throughout the summer, appear in clusters.

Calanthe vestita (in active growth)

Calanthe vestita (in flower)

Calanthe vestita

These Calanthes need filtered sunlight, warmth, and high humidity. Pot them yearly in a terrestrial compost or fir bark with shredded tree fern. During growth, do not fertilise the plants or you will burn them; give them even moisture.

Capanemia uliginosa

After new growth appears, give plants a four-week dry rest and move them to a cooler location (55°/60°F-13°/16° C at night). During the winter, resume watering, but sparingly.

C. biloba carries leaves 8-12in. (20-31cm) long and purplish flowers tinted yellow.

C. masuca has six to twelve blue-violet flowers 2in. (5cm) across. The lip of the flower is purple.

C. veratrifolia bears several small white flowers that usually have a yellow splotch at the centre of the lip. This species includes many varieties, all with somewhat different colours in their flowers.

Hint: Be sure to rest the deciduous species.

Calypso Cool 1807

This is a genus of terrestrial orchids that bear a solitary purple flower. Calypso do best grown outdoors in shade, dampness and coolness; plant the tubers in a light sandy soil with leaf mould at a 3in. (8cm) depth.

C. borialis has a deep purple flower whose lip is white dotted with red-purple. Try growing it in a pot if garden culture does not work.

C. bulbosa, similar.

Capanemia Temperate 1877

Here is a small genus of about fifteen species, all native to Brazil. The only cultivated Capanemia is *C. uliginosa*, which bears white Cattleya-type flowers whose lips are marked yellow. The scent is wonderful. Beside temperate temperatures, give this orchid plenty of sunshine, and lots of water year-round; grow it in fir or pine bark. Capanemia is perfect for window-sill growing.

C. uliginosa bears pendent scapes with small white flowers touched with yellow.

Hint: Capanemia is difficult to bring to bloom but worth your effort when it does bloom.

Catasetum Temperate 1822

This genus is comprised of more than one hundred epiphytic and semi-terrestrial orchids, most from Central America and Brazil. The flowers are possibly the most remarkable of any orchid; the colours are green, white, yellow or brown, often splotched or barred. The large light green deciduous or semi-deciduous leaves are 6-12in. (15-31cm) high. Many scented flowers appear during the spring or summer and usually last a long time.

These orchids must rest dry for about six weeks after they bloom. When flower spikes appear, do not wet them or they will rot. When the spike is well under way, resume sparse watering. Catasetums do well as houseplants, but they also thrive outdoors in the summer. If plants are outside, water them daily through the short growing season.

Catasetums will tolerate some sunlight but prefer semi-shade and warmth. Grow these summer- or winter-blooming orchids in fir bark in pots. Repot every second year.

C. cliftonii produces 3in. (8cm) waxy yellow flowers in the summer. It is easy to grow, needing no special attention.

Catasetum saccatum

Catasetum viridiflavum

Catasetum russellianum

Catasetum viridiflavum

C. macrocarpum is a large plant with many greenish yellow waxy and hooded flowers that are spotted with red.

C. pileatum bears handsome large white flowers.

C. russellianum produces 2in. (5cm), pale green flowers veined with dark green. The plant has a strong roselike smell.

C. saccatum displays lovely purple-brown flowers.

C. scurra is a small-growing species; it has white flowers.

C. viridiflavum has yellowish-green flowers with a brilliant yellow hood.

Hint: This is a complicated genus that has varied requirements.

Cattleya	Warm/Temperate	1824

The appealing Cattleya orchid should be recorded in history as the flower that launched a thousand orchids. This flower set the name 'orchid' in lights, creating a demand which rivals that for the rose. Of an exquisite and graceful shape, with flowers in appealing colours, Cattleyas are what most people believe all orchids derived from.

The genus was discovered by Dr. Lindley and named to commemorate the Englishman William Cattley of Barnet, Hertfordshire who at the time had a collection of these rare orchids. *Cattleya labiata* was the species responsible for the tremendous surge of orchid growing. According to the story, William Swainson had collected *C. labiata* in 1818 in the Organ Mountains of Brazil. Swainson did not realise that the plants were orchids or of any value and so cavalierly used them as protective packing for other tropical plants he had collected and was sending to

England. Cattley received some of these orchids and began growing them. When the orchids bloomed, so did Cattley because the flowers were unlike anything ever seen. They were large, with the typical trumpet-shaped lip, accounting for the name 'labiata' (*labium* is the Latin for lip). This orchid flower caused an immediate sensation.

However, *C. labiata* was not really the first Cattleya to find its way to England. In 1810, the Liverpool Botanic Garden received *C. loddigesii* from São Paulo in Brazil, sent

Cattleya forbesii

Cattleya aclandiae

Cattleya amethystoglossa

Cattleya guatemalensis

by a Mr. Woodforde to a Mr. Shepard at the Garden. This Cattleya was overlooked, receiving its due recognition only when Loddiges described it in his *Botanical Cabinet* as *Epidendrum violaceum*.

For thirty years after the discovery of *C. labiata*, collectors scoured the forests around Rio de Janeiro searching for that species. They did not find it, but in due course they did come upon *C. trianae*, *C. mossiae*, and other Cattleyas. This veritable treasurehouse was soon robbed by collectors as the demand for orchids in England exceeded that of tea.

So many hybrids were developed – plants of indescribable beauty – that the original species, the collector's Cattleyas, were practically lost until recently, when growers in the United States started regrowing the species Cattleya. I was amazed when I sold *C. amethystoglossa* and *C. aclandiae* in my orchid shop in Napa, California, for $100 each. Now, fifteen years later, the species Cattleya are available at affordable prices.

Cattleyas are generally medium-sized plants (to about 30in./76cm in height), with thick green leaves and pseudobulbs. They can survive much neglect and still bloom as long as they are in an airy location. In fact, this orchid prefers somewhat benign neglect rather than tender loving care. Fir or pine bark is the best potting medium, although sterile mediums such as charcoal or crushed rock

are also suitable.

These plants resent being disturbed, and repotting sets them back, so it is better to break the pots, gently crumble away the decayed fir or pine bark, and repot the plants with their rootballs intact. If plants are in plastic containers, bounce the container on the edge of a worn table to loosen the clinging roots and keep the rootball intact. The repotting procedure is difficult and takes patience.

I feed my Cattleyas in the spring, summer and autumn about every two weeks with blossom booster; the orchids bloom beautifully. In the winter, feed plants only occasionally. Year-round, keep the compost rather moist; in warm southern climates, this may involve watering every other day during the mid-summer.

Here are the Cattleyas I have personally grown and that I recommend:

C. aclandiae is a fine small growing plant with almost green flowers marked with brown and violet.
C. amethystoglossa is a symphony of pale pink; flowers are large and many.
C. citrina produces a few small butter-yellow flowers that never seem to open fully.
C. forbesii bears pale green flowers tinged brown with a pinkish lip.

Cattleya guttata 'Leopoldii'

C. *guatemalensis* bears a bouquet of small pink to salmon-coloured flowers.

C. *guttata* 'Leopoldii' produces several green flowers spotted brown with rose lip.

C. *harrisoniae* is rare and bears several fine rose-pink flowers.

C. *schilleriana superba*, a tall plant, bears fine chocolate-brown flowers with handsome full colour violet lip.

C. *velutina*, sometimes mistakenly called C. *aclandiae*, has

115

Cattleya schilleriana superba

Chondrorhyncha amazonica

yellow-brown flowers spotted purple, lip streaked with violet.

C. walkeriana is a fine winter blooming plant with large rose-violet flowers.

Chondrorhyncha   Temperate/Cool   1846
This genus of about twelve epiphytic orchids is allied with Zygopetalum and occasionally classified as Warscewiczella. These cool-growing orchids are from Central and South America. Their foliage is fan-shaped; the stunning greenish-white flowers with purple markings are produced on a short stem from the base of the foliage clump.

Plants like temperatures of about 56°F (13°C) at night and prosper in a shady location. Water carefully because too much moisture can cause rot at the crowns. Pot the orchids in large-grade fir bark.

C. amazonica has no pseudobulbs; flowers appear on short scapes from the base of the plant. The sepals and petals are creamy white, and the lip is stained purple. The orchid blooms in the autumn.

C. chesteronii has 3in. (8cm) fleshy and fragrant flowers in the summer. The lips of the flowers are fringed.

C. lipsombiae bears waxy green leaves and single white flowers stained with purple on their lips. This orchid is very fragrant.

Chysis   Temperate   1837
Six species of this strange but showy genus are available. These epiphytic orchids are native to Mexico, Central America and northern South America. The pseudobulbs are 10-12in. (25-31cm) long, cigar-shaped, and hang down over the rim of the container. Chysis are deciduous or semi-

Cattleya velutina

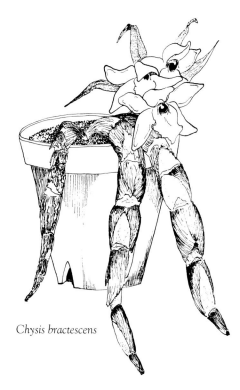

Chysis bractescens

116

Chysis laevis

deciduous, so the bulbs are bare most of the year. The varieties bloom in the spring or early summer; flowers last two to three weeks.

Chysis like two or three hours of strong sun each day. While actively growing they need lots of water and fertiliser. After the bulbs have matured, keep plants dry. At this time the orchids usually shed their leaves, and now is when it is best to move the plants to cooler temperatures at night. When new growth appears, move the plants back to a slightly warmer spot and resume watering.

Repot these plants every third year. Since Chysis dislike their roots being disturbed, dig out decayed compost with a blunt stick and replace it with fresh medium around the root ball.

C. aurea displays 3in. (8cm) diameter tawny-yellow flowers often marked with crimson. The fleshy lip is mainly crimson.

C. bractescens has three to five large and thick cup-shaped white flowers with yellow centres. The scent of the 4in. (10cm) wide flowers is powerful and spicy.

C. laevis is the handsomest of the genus, with yellow-orange fringed flowers marked red. Blooms are 2½in. (6cm) across.

Hint: Chysis grow best in hanging baskets.

Cirrhopetalum rothschildianum

Cirrhopetalum cumingii

Cirrhopetalum **Warm/Temperate** **1830**
This is a large genus of orchids, with the most species from Borneo and New Guinea. The flowers in many of the species are closely set together to form a circle or an ellipse. Plants need filtered sunlight and 70% humidity. Water the orchids heavily while they are in active growth; rest them for two or three weeks in the summer, without water. Cut back on watering in the winter also. Sometimes confused with Bulbophyllum.

C. cumingii has brilliant red and pink flowers in a half circle.
C. gracillimum bears crimson-red flowers.
C. longissimum is a remarkable species that displays an ice cream-pink inflorescence.
C. makoyanum bears delicate pink flowers.
C. rothschildianum has an umbrella of bright red flowers.
Hint: Cirrhopetalum grows best on slabs of tree bark.

Cirrhopetalum makoyanum

Coelogyne cristata

Coelogyne	Cool	1822

Ideal for growing in cool conditions, Coelogynes include about 150 species. The plants are native to India, southern China, New Guinea and Malaysia; most exist in the Himalayas. Plant size ranges from small to large; all Coelogynes are evergreen. The dramatic and prolific flowers are also long-lasting; they are usually 2-3in. (5-8cm) in diameter.

Coelogynes do well when grown in medium-grade fir bark and given excellent drainage. Water plants quite freely in the growing months (usually from early spring until summer), less the rest of the year. Feed the plants with a 10-10-10 orchid food, but avoid overfeeding, which can burn leaves. Repot Coelogynes every third year only; they dislike having their roots disturbed. Give the plants dappled sunlight, never direct sun.

C. asperata has orange markings on a white lip. Handsome flowers are carried on drooping stems, as many as twenty to a scape. It responds well to intermediate to warm temperatures, never tropical ones.

C. corrugata grows to about 10in. (25cm) and bears pretty white flowers with orange shading in the lip. This Coelogyne can take considerable neglect and still bloom.

C. cristata is seldom seen but it is a fine orchid. It has large white flowers with a crystalline sheen. Plants like night-time temperatures of 52°F (11°C). Water this orchid year-round, but feed it only occasionally.

Coelogyne speciosa alba

119

Coelogyne massangeana

C. massangeana is compact, to 12in. (31cm), and bears pendent white flowers with a yellow lip marked brown at the base. It is easy to grow in shade.

C. ocellata grows about 10in. (25cm) and has sweetly scented white flowers marked with brown or orange spots.

C. ochracea is a beautiful spring-blooming orchid bearing fragrant white flowers marked with orange. These Coelogynes like more sun than most species in the genus, but they will also tolerate cool conditions.

C. pandurata (Black Orchid) has a greenish black lip and chartreuse petals. The flowers are about 5in. (13cm) in diameter. The plant is quite a sight in bloom, growing to 36in. (91cm). It likes a shady location and plenty of water except in the winter. Grow in large containers in fir bark, charcoal or lava rock.

C. speciosa alba bears a hooded flower, making this Coelogyne unique. The flowers are tawny-beige; usually two flowers are borne on erect scapes. The plant grows to about 10in. (25cm). Its dark green foliage is quite handsome.

Hint: Coelogynes thrive in coolness.

Coelogyne pandurata

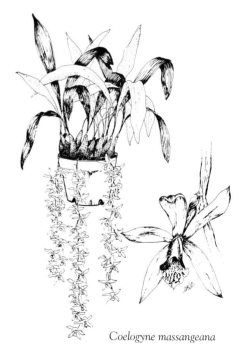

Coelogyne massangeana

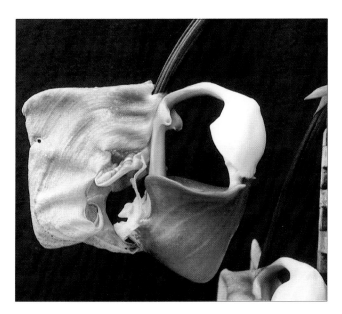

Coryanthes maculata

Comparettia   **Temperate**   **1835**
This is a genus of dwarf epiphytes from Cuba, Mexico and the South American Andes. The dramatic flowers are quite large and usually scarlet or crimson. They are difficult to grow and do best in greenhouse conditions. Keep Comparettias somewhat dry in very bright light or they will not bloom. They need 70% humidity and can be grown on blocks of wood or in 3in. (8cm) pots.
C. falcata has 4in. (10cm) leaves and vivid rose-magenta flowers.
C. speciosa has bright orange flowers.

Coryanthes   **Warm**   **1831**
With about fifteen epiphytic species from the American tropics, Coryanthes has very unusual flowers, the most

Comparettia speciosa

remarkable in the family Orchidaceae. Flowers are about 7in. (18cm) across, with a lip that contains a cup filled with liquid; this device traps insects that escape carrying pollen with them.

Coryanthes do best grown in a greenhouse, in baskets of fir or pine bark. They do not like coolness and direct sun; put them in a sheltered location. Water the orchids moderately when they are growing; rest them somewhat dry when growth is over. Plants will carry buds for months before opening, and when they open, they open all at once.
C. leucocorys has tawny-yellow flowers of typical bucket shape.
C. maculata has leathery leaves and usually yellow flowers with purple spots.
C. speciosa is a big orchid that bears three or four yellow-brown flowers with an orange lip and a tawny-red bucket-shaped lip. It blooms in the late summer.
Hint: The flowers are more unusual than pretty.

Comparettia falcata

121

Cycnoches egertonianum

Cycnoches   Temperate/Warm   1832

The Swan orchids are native to Mexico and Brazil. They produce large greenish flowers in the late summer or early autumn. Cycnoches are deciduous and have elongated pseudobulbs 4-8in. (10-20cm) long with large folded leaves. The flower scapes arch or hang in pendent style and display scented flowers that last three to five weeks. All eleven species need a warm temperature and good humidity.

C. chlorochilon has the largest flower of the plants in the genus, 7in. (18cm) in diameter. The yellow-green (almost chartreuse) flowers have a creamy-white lip blotched dark green. The morning fragrance is heavy, clean and spicy. Usually this species retains its foliage until after it flowers.
C. egertonianum has greenish-white flowers 2in. (5cm) in diameter, with a pure white or a green lip.

Coryanthes leucocorys

Cycnoches chlorochilon

Cymbidiella   **Temperate**   **1918**
This is a small group of plants native to Madagascar with large showy flowers. Plants are large as well and can be epiphytic or terrestrial. Generally this orchid does well in the temperate house with a minimum night-time 60° F (15°-16°C) and some sun. Grow in an equal mix of fir or pine bark and soil and water evenly. Only recently available, these orchids are very desirable, but I had little success with the one plant I was able to find. I believe it may have needed cooler night-time temperatures than I could give it.
C. pardelina (pardinum) was the plant I grew. It had fine flowers of chartreuse green and a large violet lip.
Hint: Try growing this plant in a slatted basket for best results.

Cymbidium   **Cool**   **1799**
This genus includes seventy species, most terrestrial and from the Asiatic tropics. The hybrid Cymbidiums, with lavish and large flowers, are the most popular, but the species are also desirable, although their flowers are not as large or colourful. The waxy flowers are small to large,

Cymbidium atropurpureum

Cymbidiella pardelina (pardinum)

white or yellow to dark purple and maroon.

Grow Cymbidiums in large pots of leafy humus. Plants prefer bright light rather than direct sunlight. They can tolerate warmth, but they need a 15°F (8°C) drop in temperature at night or they will not bloom. While these orchids are in growth, fertilise them regularly and keep them well watered except when flower spikes show.
C. aloifolum bears arching spikes of yellow flowers suffused with purple. This plant needs cool temperatures.
C. atropurpureum, a large plant, produces pendent scapes of stunning flowers; lip blotched dark maroon.
C. elegans blooms with yellow-ochre flowers in the winter. This big plant thrives in the garden.
C. finlaysonianum has yellowish-green foliage and grows about 36in. (91cm) high. In the summer it blooms with dark red flowers that have yellow margins.
C. grandiflorum has 5in. (13cm) yellowish-green flowers striped red. It produces many flowers in late autumn and the winter.
C. lowianum has 5in. (13cm) yellowish-green flowers suffused with brown shadings. It can grow as tall as 72in. (183cm).
Hint: Excellent as cut flowers; many varieties.

Cypripedium pubescens

Cypripedium Cool/Temperate 1753
These are the true Lady's Slipper orchids found in the wild in Europe and the United States. Many of the Paphiopedilums are often erroneously classified in this genus. Cypripediums have a yellow slipper and brown petals or a reddish white slipper; both species are quite handsome.

These terrestrial orchids do not transplant well, and they are not easy to grow if you buy them from a supplier. Cypripediums are an endangered species and so should never be gathered in the wild.
C. calceolus produces the typical lady-slipper shape, yellow and brown flowers.
C. insigne bears brown veined apple green flowers with a shiny texture. There are many colour variations.
C. pubescens is the most common species. It blooms with yellow and brown flowers in the spring.

C. reginae has showy snow-white sepals and petals and rose-purple lip.
Hint: This is a difficult orchid to grow in cultivation.

Cyrtopodium Warm 1813
This genus of several species is native to the West Indies and from Florida to Mexico. The pseudobulbs are elongated; the handsome large green leaves are plicated. Brown and yellow flowers appear on a tall scape in the spring.

I grew this orchid in a medium of half bark, half soil ; it responded rather well and after a few years did bear flowers, but then it quickly declined. I believe that too cool night-time temperatures did it in; it most likely would have survived only to 64°F (18°C) at night.
C. punctatum
Hint: Water this orchid copiously.

Cyrtopodium punctatum

Dendrobium aggregatum

Dendrobium   **Warm/Temperate**   **1799**

The genus Dendrobium offers an extensive array of orchids: more than 1,600 species distributed worldwide. Many of these plants are native to the Philippines, but Dendrobiums also thrive in India, Burma, Sri Lanka and China. Indeed, this genus includes so many species with so many growth habits and forms that it is difficult to discern the good growers from the recalcitrant ones.

The genus name means 'living on a tree', referring to the Dendrobiums' epiphytic habit (*dendron* is Greek for tree). *Dendrobium nobile*, one of the deciduous orchids responsible for so many wonderful cool-growing hybrids, supposedly was depicted first in Chinese drawings. The first live Dendrobium in England was brought from China by John Reeves, who purchased the plant in a market in Macao about 1837.

Another famous Dendrobium is *D. aggregatum*, which was first introduced by the Royal Horticultural Society of London; it bloomed for the first time in the collection of Mr. Harrison of Liverpool. Dr. Nathaniel Wallich discovered *D. densiflorum* in the early 19th century; it flowered for the first time in England in 1830 in the nursery of Conrad Loddiges. One of my favourites, *D. superbum*, was discovered by Hugh Cumming in Manila in 1836 and caused a sensation when it bloomed in Loddiges' nursery in 1839: the plant bore forty or fifty lavender flowers on a silver cane. My other favourite, the rare *D. victoria reginae*, I found in 1960 in a nursery. It was first described in the *Gardener's Chronicle* in 1897; it is a violet-blue flowering gem.

The genus is confusing because of the different types of growth: deciduous, semi-deciduous, evergreen, with or without pseudobulbs, with spatula-type leaves or grassy leaves. For simplicity I have classified the Dendrobiums into five groups: (1) those with pronounced pseudobulbs, (2) those with evergreen cane-type pseudobulbs, (3) those

Dendrobium densiflorum

Dendrobium chrysotoxum

with deciduous cane-type pseudobulbs, (4) evergreen cane-type Phalaenopsis hybrids, and (5) black-haired short-stemmed plants with flowers lasting two months.

To grow these diverse plants, tailor your environment to the plants. For example, type 3 Dendrobiums like a cool atmosphere of about 50°F (10°C) at night; this group

Dendrobium formosum

Dendrobium superbum

Dendrobium victoria reginae

producing this type of flowering. Flowers are large, in showy pink or lavender shades, and sweetly scented. During growth in the summer, these fine orchids need moisture and a temperature of about 70°F (21° C); when foliage has fully expanded – with a solitary leaf rather than pairs of leaves – stop watering and move the plants to a cool location (60°F /16°C) at night to induce formation of flower buds. Resume watering only when you see the nodes swelling, an indication that flowers are on the way. Repot the plants only when absolutely necessary, in loose fill material such as fir or pine bark.

Type 4 Dendrobiums (there are hundreds of hybrids) produce flowers on short stems. These Phalaenopsis-type orchids are easy to grow, prospering with a daytime temperature of 75°F (24°C), dappled sunlight, and moderate watering year-round. These plants flower for almost six months, producing one stem after the other from the tops of the canes, so do not cut off any top growth, old or new. Type 4 includes the very popular antelope-type, *D. veratrifolium*, which has small, handsome variable-pastel coloured flowers.

The flowers of type 5 Dendrobiums (*D. jamesianum* or *D. infundibulum*), the black-haired plants, sometimes last six weeks. These short-stemmed orchids have black hairy stems with white flowers spotted yellow or red. They like a cool night-time temperature of 60°F (16°C) and moderate watering all year.

includes *D. nobile*, *D. pierardii*, *D. wardianum* and *D. superbum*. Type 4 species like somewhat warmer temperatures of 55°F (13°C) at night; *D. densiflorum*, *D. thyrsiflorum* and *D. chrysotoxum* are type 4 Dendrobiums. These plants have broad and fleshy leaves and bear pendent trusses of flowers from nodes at the top of the canes. The flowers look like clusters of grapes, with perfectly proportioned lines. Give plants dappled sunlight, that is, a somewhat shady location in temperate climates. Water the plants year-round except for a short resting period (no water for about two to three weeks) before bloom time (generally the summer).

Repot type 2 Dendrobiums only every two to three years in medium-grade fir or pine bark, and feed them only occasionally because too much food can hinder plant growth. Feed twice a year in the spring with a mild fertiliser (10-15-15).

Type 3 plants produce flowers in groups of two and three from the nodes along the top of the canes; *D. nobile*, *D. superbum* and *D. pierardii* are typical type 3 plants

D. aggregatum is 4-8in. (10-20cm) tall, with vivid yellow flowers. It needs full sun and blooms in the spring.

D. chrysotoxum grows 12-30in. (31-76cm) high; it has white flowers with an orange lip. This plant needs full sun and blooms in the spring.

D. dalhousieanum is 24-72in. (61-183cm) tall, with yellow and rose flowers. It needs half-sun and blooms in the spring.

D. densiflorum grows 20-36in. (51-91cm) tall; orange-yellow flowers are produced in the spring. Plants need full sun.

D. fimbriatum is 20-38in. (51-97cm) high, with orange-yellow flowers at various times of the year. Give plants half sun.

D. formosum is 12-20in. (31-51cm) high and has white flowers with a yellow-red throat in the spring. Plants like half sun.

D. nobile hybrids are 12-36in. (31-91cm) high; in winter and spring they have blush-white flowers with lavender

Dendrochilum filiforme

Dendrochilum   Warm   1825

This is a genus of a few species from the Philippines; they are excellent plants. The clusters of green leaves are striking, and the long pendent flower spikes are crowded with white or greenish white, sometimes yellow, flowers that are quite pretty.

Plants like bright light and an average temperature of 78°F (26°C) by day and 68°F (20°C) at night. Water these orchids evenly year-round, and grow them in fir or pine bark. The flowering time is usually in the summer. Repot plants only when absolutely necessary because Dendrochilums are set back by repotting.

D. filiforme has erect leaves and many yellow or white very small flowers.

Hint: Dendrochilum needs good moisture all year

Diacrium   Temperate   1831

This is a small genus of four species native to the West Indies and Central America. The leaves are leathery and stout, and the exquisite waxy white flowers are usually fragrant. Diacriums love sunlight and water; without direct sun they will grow foliage but will not bloom. Grow these orchids in fir or pine bark; flowers usually appear from July to December.

D. bicornutum grows about 12in. (30cm) high, with 2in. (5cm) diameter white flowers that have a spotted purple lip. A healthy plant will bear as many as twenty to thirty flowers.

Hint: Diacriums are easy to bring to bloom.

tips and a lavender lip. Give plants full sun when leaves fall, half sun when they are in growth.

D. phalaenopsis is 12-36in. (31-91cm) high, with lavender flowers at various times of the year. Plants prefer full sun.

D. pierardii is 18-72in. (46-183cm) tall and has pale lavender blooms in the spring. Grow plants in half sun.

D. superbum is 24-72in. (61-183cm) high, with lavender flowers in the winter and spring. Plants need full sun when leaves fall, half sun during growth.

D. thyrsiflorum is 14-30in. (36-76cm) high, with white flowers in the spring. Plants like half sun.

D. victoria reginae is a dramatic beauty with fine reddish-purple flowers; colour variable.

D. wardianum is 24-30in. (61-76cm) high, with white-tipped purple flowers in the winter and spring. Give plants half sun.

Hint: Select the type of Dendrobiums that will thrive in your environment.

Diacrium bicornutum

Disa   Cool/Temperate   1767

These terrestrials are native to South Africa. The genus includes about two hundred species. Leaves grow in a rosette; an erect flower scape grows from the centre of the rosette. Flowers come in almost all shades, from red to pale blue.

Give plants cool, moist air, good ventilation and semi-sun. The orchids grow well in a mixture of fir or pine bark and loam, in shallow containers. Perfect drainage is a must because Disas' roots need constant moisture. After plants flower, give them a two week rest. Disas are difficult to grow, so greenhouse conditions are recommended.

D. cornuta displays green flowers marked with purple-brown at the base. The lip is white topped with purple. This 24in. (61cm) tall orchid blooms in the summer.

D. uniflora (D. grandiflora) is the best Disa. The leaves are about 12in. (31cm) long; the 4in. (10cm) diameter flowers are orange-red streaked with dark red. This is a very showy orchid.

Hint: Disas are difficult to grow under any circumstances.

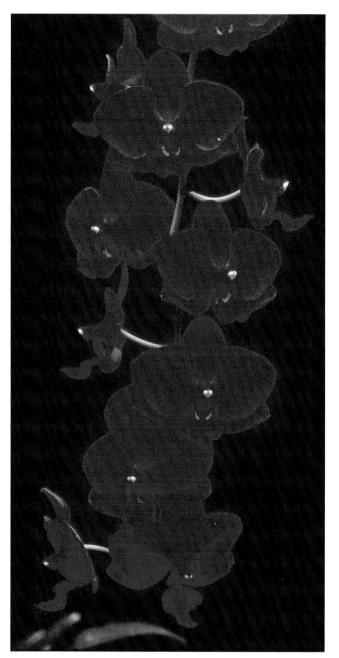

Doritis pulcherrima

Disa uniflora

Doritaenopsis   Temperate

This hybrid deserves mention because it offers so much colour. A cross between *Phalaenopsis lindenii* and *Doritis pulcherrima*, Doritaenopsis have leathery leaves and bear wands of open-faced pink or lavender flowers in the summer or autumn.

Grow the orchids in a bright location, with a rather warm

temperature of 80°F (27°C) during the day. Water plants evenly year-round, and repot them only when really necessary. Fir or pine bark is the preferred growing medium.

D. 'Asahi'

Hint: Flowers last for weeks on the plant.

Epidendrum (Encyclia)   Temperate/Warm   1753/1828

When orchids were first cultivated in England, most were thrown into the genus Epidendrum, and thus through the years the genus became ever more confusing. Now many of the Epidendrums are being classified as Encyclia as taxonomists discover or rediscover new or old differences between the two genera. For practical purposes here, I am

Epidendrum stamfordianum

Epidendrum cochleatum

Epidendrum atropurpureum

considering both genera as Epidendrums because that is the way they are generally listed in sellers' catalogues.

Epidendrum is one of the largest genera in the order Orchidaceae, but they have not been grown much, perhaps because several have small flowers. Among the more striking Epidendrums are *E. cinnabarina*, *E. prismatocarpum* and *E. atropurpureum*. Plants range from the southern United States through Central America to Mexico and the West Indies as well as on the eastern side of Peru and to some extent in other parts of South America. This wide distribution has led to varied growth: some Epidendrums have long or short pseudobulbs, whereas others have clambering stems and pseudobulbs. Some grow in areas of heat, but others thrive in somewhat cooler temperatures. With some six hundred species, the genus Epidendrum is a great treasure for growers.

131

Epidendrum prismatocarpum

Epidendrum o'brienianum

Most Epidendrums are amenable, growing under temperate conditions and a night-time temperature of about 60°F (16°C). Most are spring-blooming; a few bloom in the summer, autumn and winter. In Veitch's fine book *A Manual of Orchidaceous Plants* (1887-94), the author stated that some Epidendrums are worth while while others 'consist chiefly of species with inconspicuous flowers'. Veitch further degraded the genus by calling them weeds, but today we know differently, since Epidendrums are a vast source of flowers for collectors because they are so easy to grow.

Here are the Epidendrums that I have personally grown:

E. atropurpureum is a fine evergreen species with green and brown flowers, white lip.

E. brassavolae resembles Brassavola plants with white flowers, sweetly scented.

E. cinnabarina is tall with wonderful orange-scarlet flowers.

E. cochleatum has been in cultivation for over one hundred years; it bears small greenish-white flowers resembling a cockleshell in form. Colours vary.

E. endresii from Guatemala is dwarf and has white flowers, spotted purple.

E. fragrans has flowers that are white and streaked with crimson

E. nemorale is a stellar orchid, somewhat large with fine large rose flowers.

E. o'brienianum, a reed-stemmed orchid, produces clusters.

E. polybulbon is a dwarf plant with fine purple flowers and white lip.

E. prismatocarpum, a large plant, is very beautiful with sprays of small creamy yellow flowers marked with purple.

E. secundum bears spikes of handsome small white flowers lip stained yellow.

E. stamfordianum, in cultivation for many decades, is still popular with its small but many flowers; they are greenish spotted with purple.

E. tampense has tiny flowers and colours vary, but sprays of the flowers are quite graceful,

E. vitellinum is a must; the plant is dwarf and bears fine orange flowers. Very desirable.

Hint: These plants need plenty of water.

Galeandra devoniana

Gastrochilus bellinus

Galeandra   **Temperate**   **1830**

From Central America, these amazing epiphytic orchids display wonderful large flowers on tall scapes. Galeandras can be grown in a soil and fir bark mix. Water plants heavily in the summer; keep them a bit dry the rest of the year. Galeandras need bright light – but not direct sun – and an airy location or they will not produce flowers. After the orchids bloom in the spring, do not cut off the flower stem because often another set of flowers appears in the summer. I even had a third set of flowers once, in September.

G. devoniana grows to 48in. (122cm) in height. The 4in. (10cm) diameter flowers are brownish-purple marked with yellow; the white lip is splashed with purple. This is a stunning plant.

Hint: Keep out of sun.

Gastrochilus   **Warm**   **1825**

This genus of about fifteen easy-to-grow epiphytic species is native to Japan, the Himalayas, and Indonesia. The flowers are stunning, generally in clusters. Gastrochilus need warmth and sunshine; grow them in fir bark, and keep them moist year-round except right after they flower, at which point they need a short (three week) rest.

G. bellinus has leathery green foliage and fragrant yellow flowers splotched with purple; the lip is white.

G. dasypogon grows about 10in. (25cm) high and produces masses of beautiful yellow flowers.

Hint: Do not overwater.

Gomesa   **Temperate**   **1815**

Closely related to Oncidium, the epiphytic genus Gomesa has species that bear abundant flowers. Pot plants in fine-grade bark and place pots in sunny locations. Gomesas need a great deal of water during the summer months, but after they bloom, let plants rest for about a month. These plants are good as houseplants or in greenhouse conditions.

G. crispa, when mature, has five or six stems that bear more than 200 yellowish-green flowers that last about a week on the plant. This Gomesa is easy to grow on a window-sill or in a greenhouse.

Hint: Needs sun to prosper.

Gastrochilus bellinus

Gomesa crispa

Gongora galeata

Gongora   **Temperate**   **1794**

This atypical group of orchids includes about thirty species. The flowers are not unusually pretty; they are rather odd, being cup-like, small and borne on pendent stems. Flower colours are pastel. These epiphytes from Mexico and Central America are quite easy to cultivate, especially with cool evening temperatures. Gongoras slightly resemble Stanhopeas because of their ribbed and broad green leaves.

Keep Gongoras evenly moist; grow plants in a medium-grade bark for best results. In winter, when bulbs have stopped growing, reduce watering and keep the plants rather dry. Some species push out many flower scapes; I cut back a few of the scapes so the plants do not exhaust themselves with blooming. But this is my personal habit, not a mandate.

G. *armeniaca*, (once called *Acropera armeniaca*), has small apricot flowers borne on long pendent scapes.

G. *galeata* generally has pale tawny-yellow flowers marked with a brownish lip, but colours are variable in this species.

G. *quinquenervis* (*maculata*) is the most attractive Gongora, with tawny-yellow flowers marked brown.

Hint: Flowers appear on stems from the bottom of the container, so grow Gongoras in slatted baskets.

Grammatophyllum   **Warm**   **1825**

This small genus of large-growing plants bears incredibly lovely brownish, somewhat waxy, flowers. From South-east Asia and Indonesia to New Guinea and the Philippines, these orchids have yet to be fully appreciated. Most Grammatophyllums grow large, with dense foliage, and bear hundreds of flowers on pendent scapes, usually in the summer.

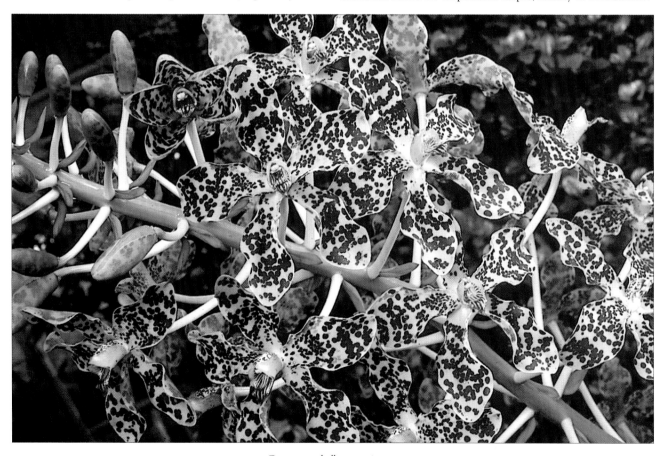

Grammatophyllum speciosum

These plants are temperamental and seem to prefer warm conditions, although the one species I grew, G. *scriptum*, did well in 60°F (16°C) during the night. I did not pamper this orchid; I let it grow almost on its own, watering it most of the year except in mid-winter.

G. *scriptum* is large, with dense foliage. Several flower scapes bloom at once, so a mature plant may have hundreds of brownish flowers.

G. *speciosum*, which I have seen growing at Selby Botanical Gardens in Florida, bears hundreds of flowers. It is similar to G. *scriptum*.

Hint: Some species grow very large, so provide ample space for the plants.

Helcia sanguineolata

Haemeria discolor

Haemeria (Ludisia)   Warm   1825

This is a genus of a single species allied to Anoectochilus and Macodes from southern China to Burma to Sumatra and Java. Grown for its handsome leaves, *Haemeria discolor* also bears bowers of fine flowers and should be grown more because it will tolerate shade and neglect and still prosper. Grow in a terrestrial mix. Bloom is in autumn or winter.

Hint: Do not overwater.

Helcia   Temperate   1845

At present there is but a single species in this genus from Ecuador and Colombia but it is such an easy-to-grow little orchid and one that has given me so much pleasure I decided to include it here. *Helcia sanguineolata* is allied to Trichopilia and has a showy small flower of yellow barred reddish-brown. Flowers arise singly but there can be several to a plant. My plant bloomed on and off through the warm months in Chicago, Illinois. This orchid likes a well-drained medium and even waterings; some sun.

Hint: Provide sunlight.

Huntleya   Temperate   1837

From Brazil and Costa Rica, this genus has become quite popular. At one time the Huntleyas were grouped with the

Zygopetalums. The flowers do not look like the familiar orchid flower; they are flat-faced, large, very waxy and brilliantly coloured. The plants grow in a fan shape with attractive foliage, but they are a bit fragile, so handle them carefully. The short flower scapes are produced from leaf axils and bear one flower, usually in the summer.

Considered hard to grow, Huntleyas actually do well in a bark kept somewhat dry rather than wet, and they like cool evening temperatures. (My Huntleyas did better in cooler Chicago than in the warm Florida temperatures.)

H. *meleagris* (*burtii*) bears a 5in. (13cm) waxy and brownish flower marked with purple 'stars'. The crest is fringed.

Huntleya meleagris

135

H. citrina and *H. lucida* (both with yellow flowers) and *H. heteroclita* (petals lined with red against a yellow background) are recent species but hard to find.
Hint: Huntleyas appreciate neglect – do not overwater.

Kingiella (Kingidium)   Temperate/Cool   1917
Sometimes classified as Doritis, this genus has one species: *K. decumbens* (*K. philippinensis*), which has delicate shell-pink flowers from June until November, one flower appearing as another one dies. The species tolerates 54°F (12°C) at night and bears abundant flowers. Pot in bark and place it where it can receive late afternoon sun. Keep the potting mix moist year-round.
Hint: Give low night temperatures.

Koellensteinia   Cool/Temperate   1854
This epiphytic genus includes ten species, ranging from Panama to the northern part of South America, including Brazil. Some species have small pseudobulbs; others form a clump of leaves. Only two species are available. This charming, somewhat dwarf, orchid bears single flowers

Kingiella philippinensis

from the base of the plant, usually in the summer or autumn.

I grow this orchid in a cool night-time temperature of 58°F (14°C) in a shady location. Grow the plant in bark and keep it evenly moist – never let it become dry.
K. graminea has grassy foliage. Flowers are about 1in. (3cm) in diameter, in yellow with purple bars and the lip a pale purple marked with yellow.
K. tolimensis resembles *K. graminea* but is a bit smaller.
Hint: Do not overwater.

Laelia   Warm   1831
Closely related to Cattleya, Laelia is a genus of about seventy species native to South America and Mexico. Laelias must have sunlight or they will not bloom. They are not particular about temperatures, even though some Laelias are classified as warm plants and listed as Schomburgkias. Actually, Laelias do very well under cool conditions, such as 50°F (10°C) at night. These orchids are ideal for window-sill gardens. Both dwarf and large forms of the plants are available.
L. anceps is medium-sized – about 28in. (71cm) in height – with a flower spike bearing several larger blooms about 4in. (10cm) in diameter. The sepals and petals are deep rose; the lip reddish-purple.
L. cinnabarina has 5 to 9in. (13 to 23cm) pseudobulbs. Several 3in. (8cm) brilliant orange-red flowers are produced from tall flower spikes.
L. crispa flowers in the summer; the blooms are blush-white with a bright purple lip.

Kingiella decumbens

Laelia anceps

Laelia purpurata

Laelia jongheana

L. gouldiana is medium-sized; it grows well in cool or warm temperatures. The large flowers are a pale rose-purple with a dark purple lip.

L. jongheana bears fine small rose-purple flowers shaped like Cattleyas.

L. pumila is small (dwarf) but flowers are large, yellow.

L. purpurata is a large plant and produces some exquisite large flowers, generally in autumn.

L. superbiens has scapes 36 to 84in. (91 to 213cm) long and bears ten to fifteen large flowers with deep rose petals and sepals. Because the plant always develops flower buds but does not always bloom, do not water it too much when it is in spike.

Hint: Laelias are more tolerant of low temperatures than we usually think, although they do prefer warmth and good sun.

Leptotes   Cool/Temperate   1833

This genus of three or four dwarf epiphytic species is native to Brazil and Paraguay. Plants do well in small well-drained containers of tightly packed bark located in a bright spot that receives daytime warmth. At night, Leptotes prefer coolness. Flowers appear in June, July, and August.

L. bicolor has one leaf that is 5in. (13cm) tall and pencil-

Laelia pumila

Leptotes bicolor

thick. The pure white flower, whose lip is stained with magenta, is about 3in. (8cm) in diameter, large in proportion to the size of the plant.

Hint: Leptotes blooms easily and the flowers last weeks.

Lycaste	Cool/Temperate	1843

Most Lycastes are epiphytic. This genus has about thirty species from Mexico, Cuba, Peru and Brazil. Because they are a bit small, Lycastes are ideal for confined spaces. They do well in temperate conditions and usually flower in the spring. Some are deciduous, others semi-deciduous, which perhaps explains their limited appeal to collectors.

Lycastes can take much abuse and still bloom. The leaves generally are pleated and paper-thin, broad and bright green; flower spikes arise from the sides of the bulbs once (sometimes twice) a year.

Grow Lycastes in medium-grade bark and give them some sun. Do not let water lodge in the young growth or rot may appear.

L. aromatica (Cinnamon orchid) is the most popular in the genus and derives its common name from its fragrant scent. The flowers are butter-yellow, about 2in. (3cm) in diameter; plants grow slowly about 2in. (3cm) high. This species was discovered in Mexico about 1826 and sent to

Lycaste aromatica

*Lycaste
gigantea*

*Lycaste
aromatica*

Lycaste macrophylla

Lycaste skinneri

the Botanic Garden at Edinburgh.

L. cruenta is similar to *L. aromatica* but has larger and more flowers; plants bear twenty or thirty blooms. *L. cruenta* was discovered in Guatemala about 1840.

L. deppei bears greenish-brown flowers with red spots. The blooms are borne on erect stems and are 4in. (10cm) in diameter. Several flowers appear one after the other, usually in the summer.

L. gigantea is rather large – to 30in. (76cm) – with persistent leaves and 5in. (13cm) diameter flowers that are pinkish-yellow. This species should be grown at slightly warmer temperatures than other Lycastes, about 60°F (16°C) at night.

L. macrophylla grows to 36in. (91cm) with brownish-green flowers about 5in. (13cm) across. This plant from Costa Rica is easy to grow.

L. skinneri is the most famous Lycaste. It is the national flower of Guatemala and is not free-flowering. If you can coax the plant to bloom, you will be rewarded with 7in. (18cm) flowers that are a beautiful blush pink. This plant likes night-time temperatures of 58°F (14°C).

Hint: Be sure to rest deciduous types – carry them dry for six weeks.

Macodes   Cool   1827

A genus of tropical orchids from Java and Borneo.

M. petola is a small plant with velvety green leaves netted with white.

Masdevallia   Cool   1794

Many of the Kite orchids are ideal sizes for window-sill gardens. The plants are native to Mexico, Bolivia, Brazil and the Andes and have remarkable flowers whose sepals usually extend into a long tail, thus giving them their common name. Masdevallias have no pseudobulbs; leaves grow from a creeping rhizome. One to four flowers per plant are either pendent or borne on tall and erect scapes, small (about 1in./3cm) or long (10in./25cm). Many species provide successive orange to almost black flowers for many months.

Masdevallias prefer shade and high (70%) humidity. Since the plants have a mountainous heritage, they can tolerate – sometimes even prefer – night-time temperatures as cool as 35°F (2°C). Keep the potting medium (rock, lava rock, charcoal or medium-grade bark) moderately moist year-round – these plants require constant moisture at the roots – and provide good air circulation. Masdevallias like a dense fog-type misting (as in their native habitat); drip

Masdevallia caudata

Masdevallia coccinea

system fog misters can be installed in the greenhouse.

Be sure the potting medium drains easily. Masdevallias prefer moderate feeding; too much fertiliser can burn foliage. These orchids bloom off old flower stalks again and again, so do not cut off old stems. Repot plants every year for maximum success.

M. *angulata* is small and bears a riot of red flowers on long scapes.

M. *bella* is about 10in. (25 cm) in height and blooms with large triangular flowers whose sepals are yellow and spotted red with dark tails.

M. *caudata* is about 5in. (13cm) high. The upper sepals are yellow, spotted and veined red; the lateral sepals are almost purple.

M. *coccinea* (sometimes called M. *harryana*) bears waxy flowers that are pale yellow to orange to scarlet or purple and 4in. (10cm) long. This spring-blooming Masdevallia is easy to grow and does well as a window-sill plant.

M. *coccinea xanthina* bears the typical kite-shaped flower, yellow, many to a plant.

M. *coriacea* needs 50°F (10°C) at night or it will not produce its purple-spotted yellow flowers.

M. *cupularis* is easy to grow and blooms with glossy chocolate-spotted brown flowers.

M. Doris is a hybrid, with delicate orange flowers.

M. *erythrochaete* grows to about 9in. (23cm), with purplish-red tails 2in. (5cm) long. The white flowers are shaded with purplish red and the white lip is shaded pink.

M. Gremlin is a hybrid with small beautiful cupped pink-orange flowers with small tails.

M. *horrida* flowers almost six months of the year. The tiny flowers are greenish- yellow and triangular, dotted with red. The leaves are 2in. (5cm) long.

M. *ignea* blooms in the spring, producing cinnabar red flowers striped crimson. This orchid grows to about 10in. (25cm) and has erect scapes.

M. *infracta* produces dozens of purplish flowers; it grows to about 6in. (15cm).

M. *peristeria* is very unusual: large green flowers marked with purple blotches. The long and stout tails are greenish-yellow.

M. *radiosa* bears successive flowers from the same stems. The flowers are dark yellow spotted brown.

M. *schroederiana* has large purple flowers and long yellow tails.

M. *torta* is quite colourful, with striped greenish-yellow flowers whose lip is purple-red and whose petals are yellow with two red lines. The column is green.

M. *tovarensis* is from Venezuela. The leathery leaves are in clusters, and the flowers, about 1in. (3 cm) in diameter, are white and waxy; they last a long time. M. *tovarensis* usually blooms in the winter.

M. *triangularis* flowers in the winter. The yellow flowers are dotted purple; the leaves are 8in. (20cm) long.

M. *xanthina* has creamy-yellow sepals, tails orange-yellow, column white with purple margins.

Hint: Grow these treasured orchids evenly moist; do not let them dry out.

Masdevallia Gremlin

Masdevallia xanthina

Maxillaria tenuifolia

Maxillaria   Cool/Temperate   1794

Epiphytic orchids, the Maxillarias comprise 300 species native to Central America, Brazil and the West Indies. They exhibit very varied growth patterns, and the colours of the flowers and the size of the plants also vary quite a bit. The rhizomatous Maxillarias need well-ventilated conditions to grow; other types thrive when grown on tree fern, with the roots exposed to the air. Most species bloom in the spring and summer.

M. *friedrichsthallii* has hooded flowers, usually yellow and they do not open fully. Summer blooming.

M. *grandiflora* has clustered pseudobulbs. It does well in a cool and shady spot and grows to 18in. (46cm). The 4in. (10cm) flowers are white and yellow, streaked with red.

M. *houtteana* produces dramatic 1in. (3cm) flowers whose sepals and petals are dark red margined with yellow; the lip is vivid yellow with red spots.

M. *luteo-alba* tolerates more sun than most of the species. The flowers are triangular, in a pretty tawny-yellow. The lip is white, the side lobes streaked with purple. This orchid grows about 16in. (41cm) in height.

M. *picta* thrives best when grown in a hanging basket. The aromatic flowers, yellow masked with purple and red petals and a white lip marked with purple, bloom in the summer.

M. *sanderiana* is the finest of the species. Keep it wet, cool, and in shade. The stunning white and red flowers, 5in. (13 cm) in diameter, stay on the plant a long time.

M. *sanguinea* blooms in the winter with yellow flowers blotched with crimson; the lip is purple-red and white.

M. *tenuifolia* has very fragrant dark red flowers spotted yellow; they are about 1in. (3cm) in diameter. The foliage is grassy.

Hint: Good group of overlooked orchids.

Miltonia   Cool/Temperate   1837

This genus has about twenty epiphytic species. Warm-growing plants (flattened pseudobulbs and yellow-green leaves) are native to Costa Rica and Brazil; the cool-growing ones are native to the high regions of Colombia. The attractive leaves are grass-like, and the sweetly scented pansy-shaped flowers are eye-catching. Most of the species produce blooms for many weeks, one flower fading before another opens.

Miltonia flavescens

Miltonia vexillaria

I grow both warm- and cool-growing Miltonias in 75°F (24°C) by day and 60°F (16°C) at night (I drop the temperatures 5°F (3°C) for the cool-loving Miltonias if they are not doing well). Plants need diffused light to bloom. About two hours of sun a day is fine most of the year, but shade plants in midsummer. These orchids also like good air circulation and 20% to 30% humidity. The flowers usually last about three weeks.

Miltonias grow year-round and need an evenly moist compost. Too much water at the base of the leaves will rot the leaves. I recommend really drenching the plants in the morning and letting them dry out during the day. I water plants twice a week, reducing the schedule to once a week during the cloudy winter months. If leaves turn yellow, the growing medium is iron-deficient; apply iron chelate once every two months.

My best growing medium is a mixture of sand, peat moss, and fine-grade bark. This denser medium encourages better root growth. Repot every year because a decaying medium hurts Miltonias. Drainage must be excellent to prevent the medium from becoming compacted. Repot into a container 1in. (3cm) larger than the old one (do *not* use big containers). Crumble away all old growing medium and put shards in the bottom of the new container. Fill the container one-third with new medium, centre the plant, and fill in and around it with the rest of the medium.

Water the plant thoroughly; let it dry out for three to five days and then resume normal watering.

Miltonias need a balanced feeding schedule because they cannot store food. Use general orchid food every third watering in all months but January and February. If your plants do not flower, add one tablespoon of bonemeal per 6in. (15cm) container to the growing medium to encourage

Miltonia spectabilis

145

Miltonia warscewiczii

flower formation. Every third month, leach out the dissolved toxic salts that have accumulated from feeding by running water through the growing medium for a few minutes.

M. *candida* and M. *cuneata* bear 2 to 3in. (5 to 8cm) chestnut-brown flowers tipped yellow.

M. *flavescens* has bright yellow flowers; the lip is marked yellow or white and blotched red-purple.

M. *regnellii* has 3in. (8cm) white flowers blotched rose at the base.

M *roezlii* displays two to five large white flowers. The lip is scalloped and stained yellow and splashed with red.

M. *spectabilis* has creamy white sepals and petals. The broad rose-purple lip is edged with pale rose or white.

M. *vexillaria* has large white or rose flowers blotched magenta.

M. *warscewiczii* bears flowers of brownish-red and rose-purple lip, small but pretty.

Hint: Miltonias dislike changes in temperature.

Mormodes   **Temperate**   **1836**
This genus includes about twenty species, most of which are epiphytes, from Mexico to Peru and Brazil. The plants need little care other than attention to resting times. The paper-thin foliage usually drops off before, at the time or

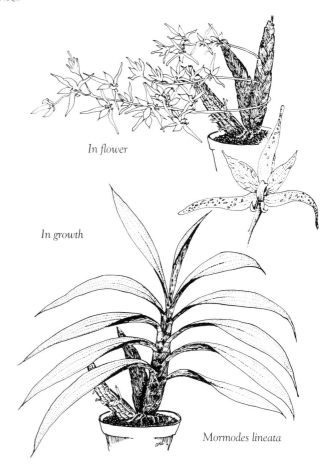

In flower

In growth

Mormodes lineata

Mormodes colossus

after plants flower, at which point Mormodes look like a Japanese flower arrangement: wands of oddly coloured blossoms on bare silver bulbs.

These orchids must rest (no water) in February and March, before they bloom, and then again for two months after they flower. While plants are resting, mist them, but again no water. Rest the plants in a shady and humid spot; after buds appear, move plants to a location that receives some bright light.

Some species lie dormant for as long as five months, so do not try to force them into growth. Mormodes do best as houseplants, not greenhouse subjects, and are virtually indestructible.

M. *colossus* has fragrant 3in. (8cm) long flowers; the sepals and petals vary in colour but usually are olive-green, yellow-brown or cream. The lip is brown, tan or yellow. The clustered pseudobulbs are about 12in. (31cm).

M. *lineata* looks bird-like, with several 2in. (5cm) flowers to a stem. The flower colour is variable; I have a plant with tawny-beige flowers, spotted red.

M. *pardina* var. *unicolor* is about 15in. (38cm) in height. The long spikes bear closely set bright yellow flowers.

Hint: For best results, rest plants for six weeks after blooming.

Notylia   Temperate   1825

A genus of inconspicuous plants but desirable because of their small size. They come from South America and Mexico.

N. *xyphorous* – single leaved with tiny white flower.

Mormodes lineata

Odontoglossum citrosum

Odontoglossum   Cool   1815

Unfortunately, if you live in warm climates, Odontoglossums are more trouble than they are worth. But if you live in moderate to cool climates, these orchids are for you because nowhere else will you find such beauty and elegance in a flower. And the large flowers are incredibly gorgeous, including the pale-pink, frilly, full-blown flowers of the famous *Odontoglossum citrosum*, and dozens of other Odontoglossums.

Characteristics of the Odontoglossums are spreading sepals and petals, a lip parallel with the column at the base, a club-shaped column and large flowers. The pseudobulbs are flattened, compressed or ovoid; most bear a solitary leaf or a pair of leaves. Leaves are laceolate and taper to a point and are bright grass-green or very leathery. The inflorescence is a scape terminating in a simple raceme or branched panicle.

The genus was discovered in Peru by Humboldt and Kunth and first described in *Nova Genera et Species Plantarum*. The name Odontoglossum is derived from the Greek, meaning 'toothed'. With some 400 species, Odontoglossums are found in Colombia, Ecuador and Peru,

with a few species in Central America. However, most are from high altitudes, where temperatures drop into the 40°-50°F (4-10°C) at night.

These wonderful orchids do like coolness, so on warm afternoons provide sufficient shade or cooling devices such as fans to keep plants in good health. Shade plants rather heavily in summer; during the rest of the year Odontoglossums can tolerate some sun, which promotes bloom.

Most Odontoglossums like to be potted tightly and resent being disturbed, so repot them only every third year. Use medium grade bark or a potting mix that does well in your area (for example, charcoal, lava rock, or cinders). Water plants year-round, but never let them get really soggy or they will rot. Also, prevent water from getting into young growth or rot may occur. Feed Odontoglossums four times a year with a good 10-20-20 orchid food, and be sure to site plants in an airy location.

There are numerous Odontoglossums, all beautiful, all with dramatic flowers. Recently, great strides have been made in the hybridisation of Odontoglossums with Oncidiums and Miltonias producing exceptionally large

Odontoglossum crispum

Odontoglossum uro-skinneri

flowers in vibrant colour combinations.

Here are the Odontoglossums I grew successfully in Chicago, which has cloudy winter days and outside temperatures often 10°F below 0°F (-22°C). It was about 45°F (7°C) in my solarium.

O. bictonienese is a fine leafy orchid that produces stems of rather small flowers, white lip and brown sepals and petals.

O. cervantesii produces some special full-faced whitish flowers marked with concentric red circles at the centre.

O. citrosum is a pendulous variety that has frilly white flowers splotched with light pink or purple at the base of the lip. There are many varieties of this plant.

O. crispum, perhaps the most popular species of the genus is an exquisite plant, bearing large white or white-tinged rose flowers spotted or blotched red or purple. Many varieties and colour forms of this popular orchid are grown.

O. lindleyanum, another fine Odontoglossum with arching stems bearing fine yellow flowers spotted red-brown towards the base, lip red-brown.

O. luteo-purpureum has very showy flowers, large, chestnut-brown and yellow.

O. pulchellum is a small plant with tiny white flowers that are delightfully scented.

O. rossii is a dwarf plant and produces small white or rose flowers spotted maroon with a broad scalloped lip.

O. uro-skinneri makes a handsome plant. The large flowers have greenish sepals and petals marked with rich chestnut-brown. The heart-shaped lip is pink, broad, and marbled white.

Hints: These are exquisite orchids for cool conditions. Do not carry them overly moist.

Oncidium ampliatum majus

Oncidium **Warm** **1800**

Often overlooked but certainly worth a spot in your orchid collection are the easy-to-grow Oncidiums. The genus, first classified as Epidendrums and discovered by the Swedish botanist Oloff Swartz, the successor to Carl Linnaeus, includes 700 species. These epiphytic orchids, which need sun, are distributed throughout Central America, Mexico, the West Indies, and parts of Brazil.

The growth habit of the genus is varied. Oncidiums may have large pseudobulbs, as in *O. ampliatum*, or no pseudobulbs but grassy leaves, as in *O. leuchochilum*. In *O. flexuosum*, the rhizome is much developed, whereas in *O. papilio* the pseudobulbs are thin, almost wafer-like. *O. carthaginense* has no pseudobulbs; *O. cebolatta* and *O. jonesianum* have fleshy leaves; *O. pulchellum* has rigid leaves.

Most Oncidiums have long and graceful flowering stems, and most of the plants bear endless flowers: I had an *O. ampliatum* that carried some 500 flowers. Most Oncidium flowers are a combination of yellow and brown, and the flowers are relatively small, as in *O. leuchochilum*, to about 2in. (5cm) in diameter, as in *O. splendidum*. When cut, the flowers last as long as six weeks; Oncidiums look beautiful when mixed with garden flowers and displayed in a vase.

Oncidiums can be grown warm or in a temperate house. They grow year-round rather than requiring a rest, so need great amounts of water during the summer months. Keep the potting medium (bark is the best) moderately (evenly) moist in the winter but never sopping wet. Most species bloom in the spring or summer; a few, such as *O. ornithorynchum*, bloom in the autumn.

As mentioned, Oncidiums must have ample sunlight to thrive. An east exposure is the best; south and west exposures will suffice, but in a north exposure the plants will not bloom.

O. ampliatum has very ovate, compressed, and wrinkled pseudobulbs. The 12in. (31cm) long leaves are very leathery, almost cactus-like. Many 1in. (3cm) flowers appear on long scapes. The plant was first discovered by Cuming in 1831 in Costa Rica and introduced by Richard Harrison of Liverpool. *O. ampliatum* generally blooms in the spring. The large form, *O. ampliatum majus*, is now available and is stunning when in bloom.

O. bicallosum is a dwarf species with small white flowers tinged yellow; occasionally brown.

O. cavendishianum is a showy species with wands of bright

Oncidium kramerianum (papilio)

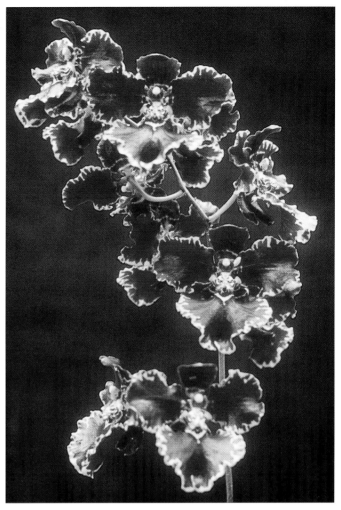

Oncidium forbesii

Oncidium sphacelatum/leuchochilum

yellow and brown flowers, hundreds to a mature plant.
O. *cucullatum* is a dwarf and, unlike most Oncidiums (which have yellow and brown flowers), this species has yellow, brown flowers.
O. *forbesii* dates back over one hundred years but it is still grown. It has terete leaves and small attractive brown and yellow flowers, many to a scape.
O. *kramerianum* (papilio), called the Butterfly orchid, produces a large yellow flower with a ruffled brown lip on long wiry stems that dance in the wind. Hence, the common name.
O. *lanceanum* is a large plant and produces dozens of small yellow and brownish-green flowers blotched with brown.
O. *ornithorhyncum* produces myriads of tiny rose-purple flowers, sweetly scented. Not showy but still worth while.
O. *sarcodes* is a fine free-flowering yellow and brown orchid.
O. *sphacelatum/leuchochilum* is large and produces dozens of brown and yellow flowers.
O. *wentworthianum* is a well-known species, popular over the years. It is a leafy plant with hundreds of flowers to a mature plant.
Hint: Oncidiums need warmth to grow well.

Paphinia cristata

Paphinia herrerae

Paphinia Cool/Temperate 1843
This small genus produces spectacular flowers. Native to South America, the exquisite flowers are somewhat triangular, with pointed sepals and petals in purple-brown streaked with white. Paphinias like dappled sunlight. These orchids need moisture in the autumn, much less in the summer.
P. cristata grows to 18in. (46 cm). It has fleshy leaves and beautiful pendent flowers that are brown streaked with yellow.
P. herrerae has large orange-yellow flowers, blotched red.

Paphiopedilum Cool/Temperate 1886
The Lady's Slippers comprise about fifty species. Growers call them Cypripediums, but Cypripediums are a completely distinct group. These terrestrial orchids are native to China, the Himalayas, south-east Asia, Indonesia and New Guinea. The plants have no pseudobulbs; some bear a single flower, others bear several.

Grow Paphiopedilums in a mixture of bark and sphagnum. Never let the medium dry out; always supply at least 60% humidity. Plants need a bright location without sun or they will not bloom.
P. argus bears in the spring one lone white flower that is striped green and dark purple. The purplish brown lip is green underneath.
P. charlesworthii is often listed as a dwarf because it is small. The single flower is mainly rose-coloured, with a yellowish-brown pouch. It likes coolness and blooms in the late summer.
P. ciliolare grows to 20in. (51cm) and bears typical Lady's Slipper orchids of dark hues.
P. concolor is sometimes classified as a miniature. The pale yellow or whitish- yellow 3in. (8cm) flowers have purple dots.
P. curtisii produces the typical Lady's Slipper flower with predominant violet colour.
P. fowliei has multicoloured flowers, erect on stems.
P. lawrenceanum, a rather large flower has the predominant

Paphiopedilum ciliolare

Paphiopedilum curtisii

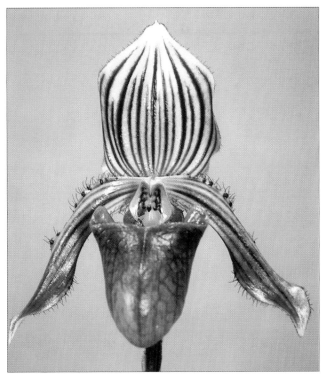

Paphiopedilum fowliei

Paphiopedilum lawrenceanum

Paphiopedilum niveum

purple colouring, veined and stained with other colours.

P. niveum has foliage about 6in. (15cm) long. The one or two flowers are satiny-white dotted purple.

P. parishii can grow tall, to 30in. (76cm), and has yellow sepals with green veins, twisted petals and is multi flowered.

P. philippinense, with glossy green leaves, bears several flowers in the summer. The sepals are white, striped with brownish-purple; petals are twisted and reddish-purple and

green. The tawny lip is marked with brown.

P. spicerianum bears one flower that is glistening white, green at the base with a purple stripe down the centre. The petals are pale green and marked with purple. This winter-flowering orchid thrives in coolness.

P. stonei has white sepals striped crimson, petals yellow with red brown spots.

Hint: Be sure the potting medium drains rapidly; use equal parts of soil and bark.

Paphiopedilum parishii

Pescatorea
Warm/Temperate   1852

Native from Costa Rica to Colombia, the genus Pescatorea encompasses about twelve epiphytes. The beautiful flowers are about 4in. (10cm) in diameter and waxy and fragrant. Pescatoreas prefer warmth, but they will adapt to some coolness, say 56°F (13°C) at night, and do well. Keep plants moist and in shade.

Grow plants in small pots of bark. Do not let water lodge in the young growths or they will probably rot. These houseplants or greenhouse subjects bloom in late summer or early autumn.

P. cerina grows about 20in. (51cm) in height. The large vibrant yellow flower hugs the rim of the pot. The leaves are glossy green.

P. klabochorum sports a very large white flower (flowers) with petals tipped purple.

P. lehmannii grows to about 24in. (62cm) with fine large flowers, white tipped with dark violet on petals,

P. wallisii, strap-leaved, tufted growth bears handsome medium-size flowers, rose lip and petals touched violet.

Hint: Do not overwater.

Pescatorea walisii

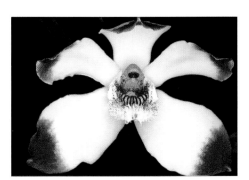

Pescatorea klabochorum

Pescatorea lehmannii

Phaius maculatus

Phaius grandifolius

Phaius grandifolius

Phaius   **Cool/Temperate**   **1790**

These terrestrial and deciduous orchids are native to China, Africa and Madagascar. Most of the species adapt to varying temperatures, so Phaius are ideal for window gardening. The leaves are often more than 48in. (122cm) in height, and the erect flower spikes display ten to twenty long-lasting, scented, and large flowers (sometimes 5in./13cm in diameter).

P. grandifolius (tankervilleae) blooms in the spring with pale flowers that darken. The sepals and petals are yellow-brown and silver; the lip is rose-purple and whitish with a blue spot in the centre.

P. maculatus produces a buff-yellow flower in the spring; the lip is marked with red on the front lobe. Dark green foliage is spotted yellow.

Hint: Phaius is generally easy to grow.

Phalaenopsis amboinensis

Phalaenopsis   Temperate   1825

From the Far East, with spatula-shaped leaves and flowers that last for months, Phalaenopsis are called Moon Flowers because the blossoms last longer than a full moon. The flowers also bloom successively; merely cut above a node after flowers fade to induce another bloom cycle.

These epiphytic or lithophytic orchids are also called Moth orchids (*phalaina* is Greek for moth), – or Dogwood orchids – the flowers of the white Phalaenopsis varieties look like the flowers of the dogwood tree. The genus has been so hybridised that there are now thousands of hybrids, with flowers in yellow to pink to lavender; some varieties even have candy-striped flowers. Phalaenopsis can flourish in low light, so they are fine houseplants.

The plants need shade, 50% humidity, and good air circulation; a steady flow of warm air is perfect. By lowering the night-time temperature to 60°F (16°C) or less in October, the plants produce more flowers. Thus I recommend moving plants to a cooler location in late autumn to encourage blooms (coolness also produces more branching). These orchids like shade, but not darkness; the light should be diffused. Direct sun in the winter is fine but not absolutely necessary; never let direct sun hit the plants in the summer as Phalaenopsis is very susceptible to leaf scorch from direct sun.

The Moth orchid must be properly watered. Plants have no pseudobulbs to store water or nutrients, so they need just the right amount of water. Too much water will make the growing medium soggy and suffocate the plant roots. Keep the medium moist, never dry and never soggy – you will have to experiment to find just the right amount. Water plants in large pots (7in./18cm or larger) twice a week in the spring and summer, once a week in the autumn and winter. Water plants in smaller pots every other day in warm weather, every fifth day the rest of the year if the weather is not cloudy and cool. If the weather is overcast, water once every seven to ten days. When in doubt, underwater. Do not let water accumulate in the crown or rot may occur.

Phalaenopsis need a good feeding regime. I recommend

Phalaenopsis stuartiana

general orchid food (20-10-10) three or four times a month in warm weather, about twice a month in cooler weather.

These orchids thrive in a growing mix of bark, crushed rock, charcoal or even broken bricks. Any mix should drain readily. I use medium-grade bark mixed with charcoal chips. Repot plants only when the mix is pulverised and brownish black (about eighteen months after potting). Be careful when repotting because the clambering roots attach themselves to almost any surface. You undoubtedly will break some roots. If necessary, break the pot to remove the plant. Then remove all old mix and trim away dead brown roots. Repot tightly; water the plant thoroughly, and then let the plant go without water for a few days, after which time you can resume a normal watering schedule. The species Phalaenopsis bloom at various times:

P. amboinensis blooms in the spring and summer with waxy 2in. (5cm) flowers that have yellow sepals and petals with narrow bars of brown.

P. cornu-cervi has barred 2in. (5cm) yellowish-green flowers; it blooms in the summer.

P. mariae blooms in the winter with 1½in. diameter (4cm) flowers. Sepals and petals are white, flushed yellow, amethyst-purple at the base.

P. schilleriana has marbled foliage and large rose-purple flowers in the winter.

P. stuartiana is another winter bloomer, producing many-flowered scapes. The upper sepals and petals are white, sometimes spotted purple at the base. The foliage is mottled.

P. sumatrana bears flowers in the spring and summer. The 2in. (5cm) flowers are near white to pale yellow; sepals and petals are barred with cinnamon to brownish-red.

P. violacea (Borneo type) flowers in the summer, producing blooms whose sepals and petals are cream-coloured, with reddish-purple on the inside.

P. violacea (Malayan type) bears 2in. (5cm) flowers in the summer. The sepals and petals are white, shaded with green, and bright violet-purple at the base.

Hint: Keep evenly moist.

Phragmipedium besseae

Phragmipedium   Temperate
1896

The twelve species in this genus are mainly terrestrial, occasionally epiphytic. The plants are native to southern Mexico, Peru, Bolivia and Brazil. The light-green foliage is strap-like, and plants have no pseudobulbs. Some of the flower petals are a striking 20in. (51cm) long. Grow Phragmipediums in a medium of perlite, shredded tree fern, and bark; never let the medium become dry. Plants need partial shade and only morning sun, along with 50% humidity. The species I grow do best in cool temperatures.

P. besseae bears a beautiful somewhat large red flower of Lady's Slipper type.

P. boissierianum has the typical twisted long petals and is yellow-green.

P. caudatum has pale yellow or white striped with yellow-green flowers, usually in the spring. The narrow petals are yellowish-white or dull brown and quite long. The slipper-shaped lip is brownish-green to bronze green, splashed with pale yellow-green. The yellowish-green foliage is clustered.

P. longifolium bears lovely waxy flowers; the petals are pale yellow-green with rose margins, and the sepals have rose veins. The bucket-shaped lip is yellow-green and dotted with purple. Flowers are produced singly, six to eight flowers to a scape, and last many months. This medium-sized orchid likes to be grown cool and wet.

P. longifolium x *schlimii*, a hybrid, has red and blush-white flowers that last for months. This is an easy orchid to grow.

Hint: Can be grown cool if necessary

Phragmipedium boissierianum

159

Pleione lagenaria

Pleione   **Cool**   **1825**

These orchids do equally well as houseplants or outdoor garden plants grown in the ground. The twenty terrestrial species are from China, the Himalayas, south-east Asia and Formosa. The flowers are mammoth for the size of the plant: 4in. (10cm) in diameter. The blooms appear in late autumn and winter.

Pleiones must have perfect drainage, so use a growing medium composed of bark, leaf mould, white sand – all in equal parts. If you plant Pleiones outside, the garden bed should be raised about 4in. (10cm) so water can run off easily. Plant the bulbs while outside temperatures are still cool, say 45°F (7°C). Most of these orchids are hardy to 32°F (0°C).

Keep newly planted Pleiones in a protected area that receives some bright light. For the first several weeks water plants sparingly until growth is well under way (roots are actively growing); then give the plants lots of water. When the leaves have fully developed (usually the end of summer) decrease watering to about once a week until buds form. Generally, foliage will die at this time, so increase watering to bring plants to full bloom.

P. formosa has 3in. (8cm) rose-purple flowers. This Pleione is a bit more difficult than the others described here, so try growing it with more sunlight.

P. humilis bears blush-white, 3in. (8cm) diameter flowers that are spotted with amethyst-purple. The lip is fringed.

P. lagenaria produces stunning rose-lilac flowers in the winter. The flowers are a bit larger than those of *P. humilis*.

P. maculata usually blooms in late October. The 4in. (10cm) white flowers have their sepals and petals streaked with purple.

P. pricei is a good houseplant because it blooms in the spring, bearing rose-coloured flowers.

Hint: Rest corms (rhizomes, bulbs) after the plants bloom. These overlooked orchids are excellent.

Pleurothallis   **Temperate**   **1813**

This genus of more than 500 miniature species is native to southern Florida, Mexico and Brazil. They are easy to grow and bloom continually throughout the warm months.

Pleurothallis platysemos

Renanthera imschootiana

Pleurothallis are epiphytes; they carry a solitary leaf, several tufted leaves, or leaves spaced on a creeping rhizome.

The plants need bright light, moderate temperatures (64°F/18°C at night), and a potting mix of bark that is never completely dry. Pleurothallis thrive as houseplants or in the greenhouse and bloom with small but pretty flowers. *P. immersa* is larger than *P. platysemos* and has succulent glossy leaves and a long scape of vivid orange, long-lasting flowers (mine lasted two months). *P. longissima* is 9in. (23cm) high, with erect scapes of whitish-yellow flowers. This is an easy-to-grow Pleurothallis. *P. platysemos* is about 6in. (15cm) high and bears tiny burnt-orange flowers on and off all summer. **Hint:** Pleurothallis like moisture.

Renanthera   Warm/Temperate   1790
The epiphytic or terrestrial Renantheras are native to China, the Philippines, Indonesia, New Guinea and southeast Asia. The flowers are red or yellow and long-lasting; they appear in the spring or summer. This genus has no pseudobulbs. The flower scape carries ten or more flowers.

The large Renantheras and hybrids need full sun all day for good flower production. The dwarfs do well in a western exposure with only afternoon sun. Repot the plants every second year in bark mixed with sphagnum moss. Give these orchids lots of water throughout the growing season; decrease watering in the winter. The larger plants need night-time temperatures above 55°F (13°C) in the winter; the dwarfs do fine with night-time winter temperatures of 55°-64°F (13°-18°C).

R. coccinea can grow as high as 84in. (213cm) and so is not suitable for indoor culture.
R. imschootiana, a dwarf, has vermilion flowers 2½in. (6cm) diameter.
R. monachica displays yellow and crimson flowers.
R. pulchella, another dwarf, has yellow flowers blotched with red.
Hint: Renantheras are usually easy to grow.

Renanthera monachica

161

Rhynchostylis gigantea

Restrepia antennifera

Restrepia   **Cool/Temperate**   **1815**
Mainly from Venezuela, this genus is fascinating. Grow the small plants in fine-grade bark; keep plants moist year-round. They need some afternoon sun and coolness (54°F /12°C at night).
R. antennifera has a single leathery green leaf. The attractive feature is the two sepals which are joined to form a single spoon-shaped pseudolip. The yellow flowers are dotted red; the lower sepals have purple stripes.
R. elegans resembles *R. antennifera* but is a bit smaller.
Hint: Grow these excellent miniatures mounted on bark or a slab of wood.

Rhynchostylis   **Warm/Temperate**   **1825**
Native to the Philippines and India, this genus includes four species. The flowers of the epiphytic Fox orchids look like the tails of foxes; they are about 1in. (3cm) in diameter, fragrant and vividly coloured, with fifty or one hundred to a scape. The fan-shaped foliage is leathery.

Rossioglossum grande

The Fox orchids are easy to grow. Repot plants only when absolutely necessary because they hate having their roots disturbed. They need warmth, plenty of sun, and heavy watering year-round. Grow them in coarse fir bark, in greenhouse conditions.

R. gigantea is big, as its name implies. The hundreds of white flowers are spotted red and quite fragrant.

R. retusa has aerial roots and leathery tongue-shaped leaves. In the summer white flowers spotted purple appear.

Rossioglossum — Cool

These orchids from Mexico were once classified as Odontoglossums. Plants prefer a sunny location and plenty of water; they thrive in large containers of bark. They can be temperamental if temperatures are too cool; do not let night-time conditions drop below 60°F (16°C).

R. grande (Tiger orchid) has succulent leaves and wands of small brown and yellow flowers. When mature, this large plant can bear as many as two hundred flowers, usually in the spring.

R. insleayi is smaller than *R. grande* but with similar flowers.

Schomburgkia — Warm — 1838

Related to Laelia and often grown under that name, Schomburgkia is a genus of about fifteen epiphytic orchids. However, their growing requirements are different from those of the Laelias. The plants range from Mexico and the West Indies to Guyana and Peru. The species include both large and small plants, with dramatic and colourful flowers (usually rose-coloured).

Schomburgkias are difficult to bring to bloom. They must have full sun most of the day, tons of water, and warmth. Do not disturb the roots; grow plants on slabs of tree fern. Some species have hollow pseudobulbs; such plants need sufficient growing space because the flower spikes are sometimes 72in. (183cm) long. The small species are also hard to cultivate.

Schomburgkia undulata

S. crispa reaches up to 36in. (91cm) in height, with 2in. (5cm) flowers that have ruffled edges. Sepals and petals are brown shaded purple, with a white lip.

S. lueddemannianii is large, with long flower scapes that bear 2in. (5cm) blooms in the summer. The sepals and petals are purple-brown; the lip is pale rose with a yellow crest.

S. splendida has spindle-shaped pseudobulbs that carry scapes of ten to fifteen brownish-purple flowers. The sepals and petals are very ruffled and edged with violet.

S. thomsoniana is about 9in. (23cm), with a pair of thick leaves. This dwarf bears 2in. (5cm) diameter rose-purple flowers in the summer.

S. undulata is the most beautiful species in the genus, with 2in. (5cm) diameter pink flowers spotted chocolate brown. The lip is white and rose.

Hint: These orchids will not bloom without sun.

Sobralia   Warm   1794

Native to Mexico, Peru and Brazil, this genus comprises thirty-five species. The growth is tall and reed-like, with tapered green leaves. The flowers are incredibly beautiful, large, and colourful (pink, purple, yellow or white shades). The flowers last only a day, but new blooms are produced successively for about a month.

Mainly terrestrial (a few grow as epiphytes), the Sobralias need to grow in rich loam, in a bright warm location with plenty of vertical growing space. Plants can grow as tall as 84in. (213cm). When the weather is hot and plants are budding, flood the potted plants and feed them regularly. When the growth is mature, keep the plants rather dry for about three weeks. Sobralias hate to have their roots disturbed, so repot them only if absolutely necessary.

Sobralia macrantha

S. *decora* is a medium (to about 24in./61cm) Sobralia that bears rose-coloured flowers in the summer.

S. *leucoxantha*, about 48in. (122cm) in height, produces large carmine-rose flowers. It is not as easy to grow as other species in the genus.

S. *macrantha* reaches about 84in. (213cm) in height and displays giant (8in./ 20cm) flowers in July. The rose-purple flowers have a flared tubular lip.

Sobralia macrantha

Spathoglottis plicata

Sophronitis   Cool   1828

True miniatures, Sophronitis grow to about 6in. (15cm) and bear scarlet-red flowers about 1in. (3cm) in diameter. From Brazil and Paraguay, the genus includes about eight species. The plants have been used extensively in hybridisation for their red colour.

Sophronitis like coolness, a bit of shade, and even moisture (do not overwater). My plants did well with very little watering except when plants were in bud, at which point they needed more moisture. The plants usually bloom in the winter.

Sophronitis coccinea

S. cernua is small, with small but brilliant scarlet flowers.
S. coccinea is somewhat larger than *S. cernua*; it bears a very showy scarlet flower.

Spathoglottis   Temperate   1825

This genus of terrestrial orchids is comprised of ten species, all native throughout the East, from Burma to China to Hong Kong and some Pacific islands. Beautiful yellow or rose-purple flowers are produced on top of erect naked stems. The foliage is tall and grassy.

Grow Spathoglottis in a rich soil laced with sand. If you grow them in pots, the plants need ample drainage at the bottom. These orchids also need good sunlight and heavy watering except after they bloom, at which time they should start a short resting period.
S. aurea blooms in the spring with 3in. (8cm) bright yellow flowers whose lip is flushed red. The leaves are 24 to 36in. (61 to 91cm) long.
S. plicata has leaves 36in. long (91cm) and in the summer bears 1-2in. (3-5cm) flowers. The sepals and petals are violet-red; the lip is bright yellow.
S. vanverberghii bears fine small bright yellow flowers.

Stanhopea   Warm   1829

With about twenty-five species native to Mexico, Peru and Brazil, the genus displays dark green foliage similar to that of the Cast Iron plants (Aspidistra). The flowers have complex inverted inflorescences that are large and vividly coloured. The taxonomy of these plants is very confusing because the flower colours are quite variable. Stanhopea was first described by Bateman in his *Orchidaceae of Mexico and Guatemala* (1837-43). *Stanhopea wardii* was introduced by Loddiges.

The flowers of the Stanhopeas last only a few days. They are produced from the bottom of the plants; large flower spikes grow vertically. The flowers have a medicinal odour (menthol and camphor). Mature plants may bear as many as twelve large flowers.

The orchids like shade and some dappled sunlight throughout the day. I grow my Stanhopeas in slatted redwood baskets and water them copiously during the early spring and summer (when bloom starts). I cut back on watering during the winter months. Plants prefer warm temperatures but can adjust to cooler (58°F/14°C) night-time conditions.
S. bucephalus is large, to about 42in. (107cm), with very fragrant variable-coloured flowers. It is often confused with *S. wardii*, but it does not have *S. wardii's* dark maroon spots.
S. devoniensis, often confused with *S. tigrina*, has a narrowly winged column. The flowers are tawny yellow to white and spotted.
S. ecornuta has flowers borne in pairs. The sepals and petals are cream-white and spotted purple.
S. insignis has a purple hypochile. The flowers are pale yellow dotted with purple and strongly scented.
S. oculata is handsome, with variable flower colour from white to pale yellow with red spots.

Stanhopea oculata

S. *wardii* has yellow or white sepals spotted red; the base of the complex lip is orange-yellow with purple spots (flower colour variable in this species).

Hints: These orchids need sun to bloom. Because the genus taxonomy is confusing, order plants by the correct species name.

Stanhopea oculata

Stanhopea wardii

167

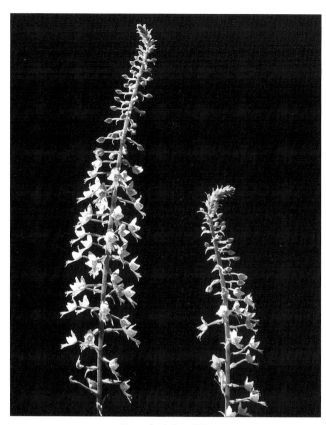

Stenoglottis longifolia

with fringed lips. The attractive foliage is curly and paper-thin.
Hint: Dry out at some time.

Telipogon　　　　　**Cool/Temperate**　　　　　**1815**
Telipogon is native to Costa Rica, Brazil and Peru. The one available species is hard to cultivate, needing care and lots of luck. These orchids must have very cool conditions, not much sun, and a very moist but airy location. Grow Telipogons only under greenhouse conditions because they will not respond to houseplant care.
T. angustifolia bears beautiful triangular-shaped yellow flowers about 1in. (3cm) in diameter. The flowers are veined with brownish-yellow and white in the centre with a dull purple spot.
Hint: Telipogon is almost impossible to bring to bloom. Try growing it in a shady spot, which may lead to flowering.

Trichoglottis　　　　　**Temperate**　　　　　**1825**
From the Philippines, Malaysia and east Asia, this genus of few species resembles Vanda. The leaves are fleshy.
　Trichoglottis like shade, with only a little sun, and need quite a lot of even watering. I grow my orchid in a combination of one-half soil and one-half bark. Flowers usually appear in the summer.
T. philippinensis produces showy blood red flowers (brownish on the inside) that last weeks on the plant.
Hint: Do not overwater.

Stelis　　　　　**Cool/Temperate**　　　　　**1799**
This genus consists of mainly miniatures. The 500 species are generally from tropical America; a few species are from Brazil and Peru. These are not as easy to grow as other miniatures, but they do produce numerous blooms once established, especially when grown as window-sill plants. Keep Stelis in a shaded location in cool temperatures (56°F/13C at night). Grow the orchids in bark, and keep them watered year-round.
S. guatemalensis grows to 8in. (20cm) in height. The flowers, small and greenish- white, are quite handsome and look like tiny tulips.
S. hymentha is not as attractive as *S. guatemalensis*. It is about 6in. (15cm) high and bears white flowers.
Hint: Fine miniatures generally easy to grow.

Stenoglottis　　　　　**Cool**　　　　　**1936**
These terrestrial orchids are native to South Africa. They thrive as window-sill or greenhouse subjects; the light green leaves are very attractive, and the small rose-purple flowers with fringed lips are quite pretty. Stenoglottis begins to bloom in October; new florets open as the spike becomes longer, so you can have a plant in bloom until January.
　Grow Stenoglottis in a mixture of loam and leaf mould; place plants in bright light with somewhat cool – 58°F (14°C) at night – temperatures. Water the young plants heavily; when growth is mature, keep the plants barely wet until growth starts again in the spring.
S. longifolia (Candlestick orchid) bears small purple flowers

Trichopilia suavis

Trichoglottis philippinensis

Trichopilia   **Temperate**   **1836**

Trichopilias are a bit harder to grow than other orchids, but their large and showy flowers are worth the effort. This genus of epiphytic orchids is native to Mexico, Cuba and Brazil and includes twenty-five species. The pseudobulbs are flat and compressed, tipped by a single leaf. The scapes are short and erect or sometimes pendent and bear one to four flowers. Most Trichopilias bloom in the early spring or late summer.

Give the plants light but not direct sun. Trichopilia require perfect drainage; they cannot stand excess moisture at their roots. Repot yearly, right after plants flower. Water the orchids carefully even while they are in active growth (I soak the plants once a week from March to November, once every three weeks the rest of the year). Grow plants as cool as possible in the summer; in the winter, keep night-time temperatures at 58°F (14°C).

T. crispa has large red flowers with a white lip spotted red.

T. elegans has white flowers about 1½in. (4cm) long.

T. marginata has rose-coloured flowers; the lip is marked inside with dark crimson.

T. suavis is about 14in. (36cm) tall. The hawthorn-scented 6in. (15cm) flowers are cream-white spotted red. The trumpet-shaped lip is spotted pink and orange.

T. tortilis has pale rose flowers about 6in. (15cm) in diameter. The sepals and petals are twisted, and the white scalloped lip is blotched red-brown.

Hint: Repot Trichopilias only when absolutely necessary.

Trichopilia suavis

169

Vanda cristata

Vanda **Warm** **1795**

The more than eighty species of these epiphytic orchids are native to the Far East, Malaysia, the Philippines, northern Australia, New Guinea and the Himalayas. Both hybrids (called Ascocenda) and species are lovely and worth cultivating. They are easy to grow in warmth (80°F/27°C by day, 65°F/18°C at night) and high humidity and usually will flower twice a year (winter and spring). (The Ascocendas grow well in cooler night-time temperatures of 58°F – 14°C.) Vandas also need free-flowing air. The flowers come in an amazing range of colours, including pale blue. The plants grow to 48in. (122cm) or more in height, with fan-shaped, leathery leaves.

Give Vandas direct sunlight and lots of water every day during their growing season. Also during the growing season, alternately feed plants with general plant food 30-10-10 and orchid blossom booster 10-30-20. It is also a good idea to mist plants (but not the leaves – aim the spray at the container and growing medium) in the summer because Vandas love a saturated atmosphere.

Do not repot Vandas too often because they have numerous aerial roots that may break. Grow Vandas in large containers, preferably open baskets, in large-grade bark; replenish the top 4in. (10cm) of bark every year.

Vanda merrillii

Vanilla planifolia

Vanda tricolor

Note that you should not use redwood baskets because the wood exudes a sap that harms the Vandas. Also avoid plastic containers, which hold moisture too long.

V. cristata is about 9in. (23cm) tall. The 2in. (5cm) flowers have yellowish-green sepals and petals; the lips are streaked with red and white lines. Flowers last more than two months.

V. merrillii bears handsome cream-yellow flowers blotched red.

V. parishii bears fragrant yellowish-green flowers that are spotted red-brown. The leaves are 6 to 9in. (15 to 23cm) long.

V. roxburghii grows to about 24in. (61cm). This easy-to-grow Vanda will bear aromatic pale green flowers splotched brown. The small lip is lined white and has a violet-purple disc.

V. sanderiana (Queen of the Vandas) has flowers almost 5in. (13cm) in diameter. The blooms are soft pink suffused with white, the lower petals yellow crossed with red veins. The intricate lip is tawny-yellow streaked red, the front part marked chocolate brown.

V. tricolor, strapleaved with medium size white flower spotted red.

Hint: The Vandas must have plenty of light.

Vanilla   **Warm**   **1799**
One of the species – *V. planifolia* – is one of the few orchids used commercially. The genus is from the West Indies; plants are vining, with beautiful yellow flowers. The vanilla flavouring is extracted from the pods (vanilla is also made synthetically.) The plant has fleshy leaves and does not bloom until it is mature (about seven years). Plants usually bloom in the summer; I have seen only a few in bloom in various conservatories.

172

Xylobium squalens

Vanilla needs warmth and excellent sun or it will not prosper. The plant was first mentioned in Andrews' *Botanical Repository* and introduced into England about 1810.

V. *planifolia* is a handsome vine with pale green fleshy leaves and yellowish green flowers. It will grow in a medium or pinned to a trellis. It is difficult to cultivate. A variegated type is also available.

V. *pompona* is similar to V. *planifolia* but not as large.

Hint: Vanilla does not bloom until it is mature, so do not try to force bloom.

Xylobium   Temperate   1825
These epiphytic orchids from Peru, the West Indies and Brazil are grouped into twenty species. The plants bear many fragrant flowers in pastel shades of green, yellow or white.

The species from Central America (X. *elongatum*, X. *squalens*) must have warmth and sun; those from the cooler countries thrive in semi-shade. All Xylobiums need a rest before and after flowering. Grow the orchids in bark, in small containers. Water plants heavily when they are growing, less the rest of the year. Xylobiums usually bloom in the spring, but some of mine have produced blooms in late autumn.

X. *bractescens* need coolness at night, about 56°F (13°C). The 3in. (8cm) diameter flowers have light sepals and petals blotched purple-brown, with a broad white lip.

X. *elongatum* has pale yellow flowers; the lip is generally purple. The glossy green leaves are about 1½in. (4cm) in length.

X. *squalens* has egg-shaped pseudobulbs. The waxy tawny-beige flowers are borne on hanging scapes.

Zygopetalum intermedium

Zygopetalum mackayi

Zygopetalum Cool 1827

In the past few years this orchid has become a favourite of collectors. The twenty-five species grow from Venezuela to Brazil, as terrestials or epiphytes. They have often been confused with other genera. The exquisite flowers are blue and brown and appear in the summer or winter.

Zygopetalums must be grown in a somewhat shady

174

Zygopetalum labiosum

location. They need very even watering; too much moisture many kill them, and too little will prevent blooms. Recently these orchids have been hybridised to produce plants somewhat easier to care for.

Z. *candidum* has 2in. (5cm) flowers with white sepals and petals and a purple lip.

Z. *crinitum* has brown, blue, and green flowers on pendent scapes.

Z. *intermedium* bears the typical Zygopetalum flowers: brownish-purple with white lip. Colours variable.

Z. *labiosum* has large flowers, white, with violet veins and brown petals.

Z. *mackayi* is large and the most popular Zygopetalum grown. This hybrid has 3in. (8cm) brownish purple flowers with a white and purple lip and beautifully scalloped.

Hint: Keep plants evenly moist.

Dendrobium nobile

～ APPENDIX 1 ～
Quick Reference Chart

This chart includes 90 genera and some 350 species; all are noted in greater detail in Chapter 8 Gallery of Orchids.

Plant size categories

MN (miniature)	to 8in. (20cm)
S (small)	9 to 14in. (23 to 36cm)
M (medium)	15 to 30in. (38 to 76cm)
L (large)	31in. and over (79 cm)

Flower Size

S	to 1in. (3cm)
M	2 to 3 inches (5 to 8cm)
L	4 and over inches (10cm)

Bloom Time abbreviations:

spring	sp
summer	s
autumn	a
winter	w
various	v

Exposure times:

full sun	6 to 7 hours
half sun	2 to 3 hours
broken sun	4 to 6 hours
shade	light, no sun
semi-shade	1 to 2 hours

Note: Plant size and flower colour, size and bloom time may vary depending upon growing media, climate and how the plant is grown. The information given here is a general guide and is based on the author's collection grown in average day temperatures of 78ºF and 10ºF lower at night.

Name	Plant Size	Flower Colour	Flower Size	Bloom Time	Exposure
Acampe					
pachyglossa	M	yellow, red	S	sp	half sun
papillosa	M	yellow, red	S	v	half sun
Acanthophippium					
montianianum	L	yellow, red	M	s	half sun
Acineta					
chrysantha (densa)	M	yellow, red	M	sp	half sun
superba	M	pale yellow	M	sp/s	shade

Name	Plant Size	Flower Colour	Flower Size	Bloom Time	Exposure
Aerangis					
biloba	S	white	S	v	half sun
fastuosa	S	white	S	v	half sun
kirkii	S	white	S	s	half sun
kotschyana	M	white	M	s	half sun
rhodostica	S	white	S	sp	half sun
Aerides					
crassifolium	MN/S	purple	S	s	half sun
japonicum	MN	white, red	S	s	half sun
odoratum	S/L	rose, white	S	v	full sun
Angraecum					
compactum	MN	white	S/M	a	shade
eburneum	M	white	M	w	half sun
eichlerianum	M/S	white	M	w	shade
falcatum (Neo-finetia falcata)	MN	white	S	v	shade
leonis	MN	white	M	a/w	shade
sesquipedale	M/L	white	L	w	semi-shade
veitchii	M/L	white	L	w	semi-shade
Anguloa					
cliftonii	M	golden-yellow, purple-brown	L	s	half sun
clowesii	M/L	yellow, orange	L	s	half sun
ruckeri	L	orange-red	L	s	half sun
uniflora	L	white, pink	M	sp/s	half sun
Ansellia					
africana (gigantea)	M	yellow-brown	S/M	s	half sun
Arachnis					
clarkei	L	yellow, brown	M	s	sun
flos-aeris (moschifera)	L	greenish-white, yellow	L	s	sun
Arpophyllum					
spicatum	L	pink	S	s	sun
Arundina					
graminifolia	L	rose	M	s	sun

Name	Plant Size	Flower Colour	Flower Size	Bloom Time	Exposure
Ascocentrum					
ampullaceum	S	rose-carmine	S	sp	sun
curvifolium	S	red	S	sp	half sun
micranthum	S	white, lavender	S	sp	sun
miniatum	MN	orange	S	sp	full sun
pumilum	MN	lavender	S	sp	full sun
Barkeria					
lindleyana	M	lilac	M	s	half sun
skinneri	M	lilac	M	s	half sun
Bifrenaria					
harrisoniae	M	white, yellow, reddish-purple	M/L	s	half sun
tyrianthina	M	reddish-purple, deep purple	M/L	s	half sun
Bletia					
gracilis	M	purple-rose	S/M	s	half sun
purpurea	M	rose	S	s	half sun
shepherdii	M	pink	S	s	half shade
sherratiana catenulata	M	rosy-red	S	s	half sun
striata		rose-pink	S	s	half sun
Bletilla					
lindeyana	S	violet	S	s	half sun
purpurea	S	rose	S	s	half sun
skinneri	S	rose, purple	M	s	half sun
Bollea					
coelestis	M	violet, white	L	a/w	shade
ecuadoriana	M	violet-red	L	a	shade
violacea	M	white, violet-blue	L	a	shade
Brassavola					
cucullata	MN	white	M	v	full sun
digbyana (Rhyncholaelia digbyana)	MN/M	pale green	L	v	full sun
glauca alba	MN/S	white	M	sp	half sun
nodosa	MN	pale green	M	v	full sun
Brassia					
caudata	M	light green, spotted	L	v	full sun
gireoudiana	M	greenish-yellow, brown	L	v	full sun
longissima	M	yellow spotted brown	L	s	

Name	Plant Size	Flower Colour	Flower Size	Bloom Time	Exposure
maculata	M	greenish-yellow, brown	L	s	full sun
verrucunda	M	white, greenish-brown	L	s	full sun
Bulbophyllum					
barbigerum	MN	purple-brown	S	s	half sun
grandiflorum	S	tawny-beige	M	v	half sun
lemniscatoides	MN	purple	S	v	half sun
lobbii	S	brownish-yellow	S	s	shade
medusae (Cirrho-petalum medusae)	S	straw coloured	S	v	half sun
morphologorum	M	yellowish-brown	S	v	shade
rothschildianum	S	red flowers, striped darker	S	v	shade
Calanthe					
biloba	S/M	purple, yellow	S	s	broken sun
labrosa	S	rose-purple	S	w	broken sun
masuca	M	violet-blue	M	s	broken sun
rosea	S	pale pink	S	w	half sun
veratrifolia	M	white	S	v	half sun
vestita	S	white, pink	M	w	half sun
Calypso					
borialis		deep purple			
bulbosa	S	purple	S	v	shade
Capanemia					
uliginosa	S	white, yellow	S	v	half sun
Catasetum					
cliftonii	M	yellow	M	s	half sun
macrocarpum	L	greenish-yellow	M	sp	half sun
pileatum	M	white	L	a	half sun, then full
russellianum	M	pale green, dark green	M	s, a	half sun, then full
saccatum	M	purple-brown	S	s	half sun
scurra	MN	white	S	sp	half sun, then full
viridiflavum	S	yellow-green	M	s	half sun, then full
Cattleya					
aclandiae	M	green, brown, violet	M	s	full or half sun

Name	Plant Size	Flower Colour	Flower Size	Bloom Time	Exposure
amethystoglossa	M	pink	M	v	half sun
citrina	MN/S	yellow	S	sp, s	full or half sun
forbesii	M	pale green	M	v	sun
guatemalensis	M	variable	S	v	half sun
guttata 'Leopoldii'					
harrisoniae	M	rose-violet	M	v	half sun
schilleriana superba	M	brown, violet	M	s	half sun
velutina	M	yellow-brown, violet,	M	s	half sun
walkeriana	MN	rose-violet	L	w	half sun
Chondrorhyncha					
amazonica	M	white, purple	M	a	half sun
chesteronii	M	greenish-white	M	a	half sun
lipsombiae	M	white, purple	M	v	half sun
Chysis					
aurea	S/L	tawny-yellow	M	v	half sun
bractescens	S/M	white, yellow	L	sp	half sun
laevis	S/M	yellow-orange	M	sp	half sun
Cirrhopetalum					
cumingii	MN	red, pink	S	v	broken sun
gracillimum	MN	crimson-red	S	v	half sun
longissimum (*rothschildiana*)	MN	variable	L	w	broken sun
makoyanum	MN	pink	S	v	shade
roxburghii	MN	pink	S	v	shade
Coelogyne					
asperata	S	white, orange	M	sp	half sun
corrugata	S	white, orange	M	sp	half sun
cristata	M	white	L	w, sp	semi-shade
massangeana	S	white, brown	M	v	semi-shade
ocellata	S	white, orange	S	sp	half sun
ochracea	M	white, orange	S	sp, s	half sun
pandurata	L	chartreuse, black	L	s	half sun
speciosa alba	S	tawny-beige	L	v	semi-shade
Comparettia					
falcata	MN/S	rose-magenta	S	s	half sun
speciosa	MN/S	orange	S	s	half sun

181

Name	Plant Size	Flower Colour	Flower Size	Bloom Time	Exposure
Coryanthes					
leucocorys	M	tawny-yellow	L	v	half sun
maculata	M	yellow, purple	L	v	half sun
speciosa	M	yellow-brown	L	v	half sun
Cycnoches					
chlorochilon	S/M	yellow-green	L	v	half sun
egertonianum	S/M	greenish-white	S	s	half sun
Cymbidiella					
pardelina (pardinum)	M	variable	L	v	shade
Cymbidium					
aloifolium	M/L	yellow, purple	M	a/w	half sun
atropurpureum	M/L	maroon	M	w	half sun
elegans	M/L	yellow-ochre	S	s	half sun
finlaysonianum	M/L	dark red	S	s	half sun
grandiflorum	M/L	yellowish-green, red	L	v	half sun
lowianum	M/L	yellowish-green, brown	L	w	half sun
Cypripedium					
calceolus	S	yellow, brown	M	sp	shade
insigne	S	yellow, brown	M	sp	shade
pubescens	S	yellow, brown	M	sp	shade
reginae	S	white, rose	M	sp	shade
Cyrtopodium					
punctatum	L	brown, yellow	L	s	full sun
Dendrobium					
aggregatum	MN	yellow	S	sp	full sun
chrysotoxum	S/M	yellow	S	sp	full sun
dalhousieanum	M/L	yellow, rose	M	sp	half sun
densiflorum	M/L	orange-yellow	S	sp	full sun
fimbriatum	M/L	orange-yellow	M	v	half sun
formosum	S/M	white	M	sp	full sun
nobile	S/M	lavender	M	a/w	shade
phalaenopsis	S/L	lavender	M	v	full sun
pierardii	M/L	pink	M	sp	half sun
superbum	L	lilac-rose	M	sp	half sun
thyrsiflorum	M	white, with orange lip	M	s	half sun
victoria reginae	S	white streaked violet	M	s/a	shade
wardianum	M	violet flowers	M	s/a	shade

Name	Plant Size	Flower Colour	Flower Size	Bloom Time	Exposure
Dendrochilum					
filiforme	M/L	yellow	S	s	half sun
Diacrium					
bicornutum	M	white	M	s	half sun
Disa					
cornuta	M	green, purple-brown	M	s	shade
uniflora (grandiflora)	M	orange, red	M	s	shade
Doritaenopsis					
'Asahi'	M	pink	M	v	half sun
Epidendrum (Encyclia)					
atropurpureum	M	green, white, brown	M	sp	full sun
brassavolae	S	white	S	v	half sun
cinnabarina	M	orange-scarlet	S	s	full sun
cochleatum	S	greenish-white	S	v	full sun
endresii	S	white	S	v	half sun
fragrans	S	white	M	s	half sun
nemorale	S	rose	M	w	full sun
o'brienianum	M/L	orange	S	v	half sun
polybulbon	S	purple, white	S	a	half sun
prismatocarpum	M/L	yellow, purple spots	M	s	full sun
secundum	S	red	M	s	sun
stamfordianum	M/L	greenish, purple	S	sp	half sun
tampense	M	variable	S	s	full sun
vitellinum	M	orange	S	w	broken sun
Galeandra					
devoniana	L	brownish-purple	L	s	half sun
Gastrochilus					
bellinus	S	yellow	S	s	half sun
dasypogon	S	yellow, brown, red	S	s	half sun
Gomesa					
crispa	MN/S	yellowish-green	S	v	half sun
Gongora					
armeniaca	S	apricot	S	s	broken sun
galeata	S	tawny-yellow	S	v	broken sun

Name	Plant Size	Flower Colour	Flower Size	Bloom Time	Exposure
quinquenervis (*maculata*)	M	tawny-yellow, brown	S	v	half sun
Grammatophyllum					
scriptum	L	brown	M	s	shade
speciosum	L	brown	M	s	shade
Haemeria (Ludisia)					
discolor	S/M	white	S	s	shade
Helcia					
sanguineolata	S	yellow, brown	S	v	broken sun
Huntleya					
citrina	M	yellow	L	s	shade
heteroclita	M	red, yellow			
lucida	M	yellow	L	s	shade
meleagris (*burtii*)	M	brownish	L	v	shade
Kingiella (Kingidium)					
decumbens (*philippinensis*)	MN	pink	S	v	broken sun
Koellensteinia					
graminea	MN	yellow, brown	S	a/w	broken sun
tolimensis	MN	yellow, brown	S	a/w	broken sun
Laelia					
anceps	M	rose	L	s	half sun
cinnarbarina	M	orange-red	M	s	half sun
crispa	M	blush-white, purple	M	s	half sun
gouldiana	M	rose-purple	M	s	half sun
jongheana	MN	rose-purple	S	v	half sun
pumila	S	pink	M	a	sun
purpurata	L	white, purple	L	s	half sun
superbiens	L	rose	L	s	full sun
Leptotes					
bicolor	MN	white stained red	M	s	broken sun
Lycaste					
aromatica	S/M	yellow	M	w	broken sun; semi-shade when leaves fall

Name	Plant Size	Flower Colour	Flower Size	Bloom Time	Exposure
cruenta	S/M	yellow	M	w	dappled sun
deppei	M	greenish-brown, red spots	L	w	broken sun; semi-shade when leaves fall
gigantea	M	pinkish-white	L	a/w	broken sun
macrophylla	M	olive-green, pink spots	M	s	half sun
skinneri	M	rose	L	v	broken sun
Macodes	S	multicoloured foliage, reddish brown	S	v	shade
petola					
Masdevallia					
angulata	S/M	red	S	s	shade
bella	S	yellow, red	S	v	shade
caudata	S	yellow, red	S	s	shade
coccinea (harryana)	S	red	S	s	shade
coccinea xanthina					
coriacea	S	yellow, purple spotted	S	v	half sun
cupularis	S	brown, chocolate	S	v	half sun
Doris	S	orange	S	v	half sun
erythrochaete	S	white, purplish-red	S	v	half sun
Gremlin	S	pink-orange	S	v	half sun
horrida	S	greenish-yellow, red	S	v	shade
ignea	M	red	S	v	broken sun
infracta	MN	purple	S	s	half sun
peristeria	S	green	M	v	half sun
radiosa	S	yellow, brown	S	v	half sun
schroederiana	S	purple	M	s	half sun
torta	S	greenish-yellow	S	s	shade
tovarensis	S	white	S	v	shade
triangularis	M	yellow	S	v	half sun
xanthina	S	yellow, violet	S	a	half sun
Maxillaria					
friedrichsthalii	M	yellow	M	w	half sun
grandiflora	M	white, yellow, red	L	w	broken sun
houtteana	M	red	S	a/w	broken sun
luteo-alba	M	yellow, white	M	a/w	broken sun
picta	S	yellow	S	v	broken sun
sanderiana	M	white, red	L	s	half sun
sanguinea	M	yellow, red	M	a/w	half sun
tenuifolia	M	red, yellow	S	s	half sun

Name	Plant Size	Flower Colour	Flower Size	Bloom Time	Exposure
Miltonia					
candida, cuneata	S/M	brown, yellow	M	a	broken sun
flavescens	S/M	yellow		s	broken sun
regnellii	S/M	white	M	v	broken sun
roezlii	S/M	white	L	sp, a	broken sun
spectabilis	S	white	M	s	half sun
vexillaria	S/M	white, rose	M	sp	half sun
warscewisczii	S/M	brownish-red, rose-purple	M	sp	half sun
Mormodes					
colossus	M	olive-green or yellow	M	a, w	half sun; broken sun when leaves fall
lineata	M	tawny-brown	S	w	half sun; broken sun when leaves fall
pardina var. *unicolor*	M	yellow	L	a/w	half sun
Notylia					
barkeri	MN/S	white, purple	S	s	full sun
xyphorous	MN/S	purple	S	s	full sun
Odontoglossum					
bictoniense	M	brown, white	S	v	shade
cervantesii	M	white, red	S	sp	half sun
citrosum	M	white, pink, purple	M	v	semi-shade
crispum	M	white, rose	L	w	semi-shade
lindleyanum	M	yellow	M	w	semi-shade
luteo purpureum	M	brown	M	a/w	semi-shade
pulchellum	S	white	S	sp	broken sun
rossii	MN	white, rose	S	v	broken sun
uro-skinneri	M/L	brown, pink	L	sp	half sun
Oncidium					
ampliatum	M	yellow	S	a	sun
bicallosum	S	whitish-yellow, brown	S	s	full sun
cavendishianum	M	yellow, brown	S	v	half sun
cucullatum	S	yellow, brown	S	v	full sun
forbesii	S	yellow, brown	S	s	full sun
kramerianum (*papilio*)	S	yellow, brown	M	s/s	half sun
lanceanum	M	yellow, brown	S	s	broken sun
ornithorynchum	M	pink	S	a, w	half sun
sarcodes	S/M	yellow, brown	S	v	broken sun
sphacelatum/ leuchochilum	M/L	yellow, brown	S	sp	broken sun

Name	Plant Size	Flower Colour	Flower Size	Bloom Time	Exposure
wentworthianum	S/M/L	yellow, brown	S	v	half sun
Paphinia					
cristata	S	brown	S/M	v	semi-shade
herrerae	S	orange-yellow	S/M	v	semi-shade
Paphiopedilum					
argus	M	white, purplish brown, green	M	w	semi-shade
charlesworthii	S	rose, brown	L	w	semi-shade
ciliolare	M	variable	M	v	semi-shade
concolor	MN/S	whitish-yellow	M	sp	half sun
curtisii	M	violet	M	s	half sun
fowliei	M	variable	M	v	half sun
lawrenceanum	M	purple veined	M	v	semi-shade
niveum	S	white dotted purple	S	s	half sun
parishii	M	yellow sepals, green	M	v	semi-shade
philippinenses	M	reddish-purple, green	M	v	semi-shade
spicerianum	M	variable	M	v	semi-shade
stonei	M	white, pink, brown	M	s	half sun
Peristeria					
alata (elata)	L	yellowish	M	s	broken sun
Pescatorea					
cerina	M	yellow	L	s	half sun
klabochorum	M	white tipped purple	L	v	half sun
lehmanni	M	white tipped violet	L	v	half sun
wallisii	M	rose, violet	L	v	half sun
Phaius					
grandifolius (*tankervilleae*)	M/L	yellow-brown, silver	L	sp, s	broken sun or semi-shade
maculatus	M/L	yellow	M	sp	broken sun
Phalaenopsis		(leaf spread)			
amboinensis	M	yellow, brown	M	w	semi-shade
cornu-cervii	S	yellow, green	M	w	semi-shade
mariae	S	white, yellow	S	v	semi-shade
schilleriana	M	rose-purple	L	w	broken sun
stuartiana	M	white spotted purple	M	sp	broken sun
sumatrana	S	yellow barred with brown	M	s	broken sun
violacea (Borneo)	M	cream, reddish-purple	M	v	broken sun
violacea (Malayan)	M	white shaded green, rose	M	s	broken sun

Plant Name	Flower Size	Flower Colour	Bloom Size	Time	Exposure
Phragmipedium					
besseae	M	deep red	M	v	shade
boissierianum					
caudatum	M	variable	L	a	half sun
longifolium		variable	L	v	half sun
longifolium x *schlimi*	M	red, blush-white	M	s	half sun
Pleione					
formosa	M	rose-purple	L	v	semi-shade
humilis	S	blush-white	M	v	semi-shade
lagenaria	S	rose, lilac	L	v	semi-shade
maculata	S	white	L	a	broken sun
pricei	MN	rose	L	sp	broken sun
Pleurothallis					
immersa	MN	orange	S	s	half sun
longissima	MN/S	whitish-yellow	S	v	half sun
platysemos	MN	orange	S	v	half sun
Renanthera					
coccinea	L	red	S	a/w	semi-shade
imschootiana	M	red	M	s	half sun
monachica	M	yellow, crimson	S	a/w	semi-shade
pulchella	MN	yellow, red	S	s	full sun
Restrepia					
antennifera	MN	yellow	S	v	semi-shade
elegans	MN	yellow	S	v	semi-shade
Rhynchostylis					
gigantea	M	white spotted purple	M	s	half sun
retusa	M	white spotted purple	M	s	half sun
Rossioglossum					
grande	M/L	brown, yellow	L	s	half sun
insleayi	M	brown, yellow	M	s	broken sun
Schomburgkia					
crispa	L	brown, purple	M	s	full sun
lueddemannianii	L	purple-brown	M	v	full sun
splendida	L	brownish-purple	M	s	full sun
thomsoniana	L	rose-purple	M	s	half sun
undulata	L	pink	M	s	half sun

Name	Plant Size	Flower Colour	Flower Size	Bloom Time	Exposure
Sobralia					
decora	M	rose	L	s	full sun
leucoxantha	L	rose	L	s	full sun
macrantha	L	rose-purple	L	s	full sun
Sophronitis					
cernua	MN	red	S	w	semi-shade
coccinea	MN	red	S/M	w	semi-shade
Spathoglottis					
aurea	M	yellow	M	sp	half sun
plicata	M/L	red, yellow	S	sp	half sun
vanverberghii	M	yellow	S	sp	half sun
Stanhopea					
bucephalus	L	variable, orange spotted	L	s	full sun
devoniensis	L	yellow, white	L	s	full sun
ecornuta	M/L	white, purple	L	s	shade
insignis	M/L	yellow	L	s	shade
oculata	M/L	white, pale yellow	L	s	shade
wardii	L	white, purple	L	s	sun
Stelis					
guatemalensis	MN	greenish-white	S	v	half sun
hymentha	MN	white	S	v	half sun
Stenoglottis					
longifolia	S/M	purple	S	w	half sun
Telipogon					
angustifolia	MN	yellow veined, brownish-yellow	S	s	half sun
Trichoglottis					
philippinensis	M	red	M	v	semi-shade
Trichopilia					
crispa	S	red, white	L	sp, s	half sun
elegans	S	white	M	sp, s	half sun
marginata	S	rose	L	sp, s	half sun
suavis	S	cream, red	L	sp, s	half sun
tortilis	M	pink, blotched	L	s	half sun
Vanda					
cristata	S	yellowish-green, red	M	a, w	full sun

Name	Plant Size	Flower Colour	Flower Size	Bloom Time	Exposure
merrillii	M	yellow, red	M	a	full sun
parishii	M	yellowish-green, red	L	a	full sun
roxburghii	M	pale green, brown	L	w	full sun
sanderiana	L	pink, white	L	w	half sun
tricolor	L	white, red	M	w	half sun
Vanilla					
planifolia	L	yellowish-green	L	s	broken sun
pompona	L	yellow	L	s	broken sun
Xylobium					
bractescens	M	purple-brown	M	s	half sun
elongatum	M	pale yellow	M	v	half sun
squalens	M	tawny-beige	M	a	half sun
Zygopetalum					
candidum	M	white, purple	M	w	semi-shade
crinitum	M	blue, green	M	w	semi-shade
intermedium	M	brownish-purple	M		shade
labiosum	M	white, brown, violet	L	w	semi-shade
mackayi	M	brownish-purple	L	w	semi-shade

~ APPENDIX 2 ~
The Classification of Orchids

Within the orchid family, genera and their species are called subtribes. The classification system R.A. Dressler proposed in 1974 is the one most orchid authorities consider 'correct'.

The following is a listing of the principal genera and their main attributes.

Acampe. This African and Asian genus of epiphyte orchids contains about twelve species. The fleshy flowers are borne in clusters; leaves are leathery.

Acanthophippium. This is a genus of mostly terrestrial orchids. The somewhat large plants (to 40in./102cm high) have broad leaves and colourful tulip-shaped blooms.

Acineta. With more than twelve species, this genus of epiphytes ranges from Mexico to South America. The flower spikes grow straight downward from the base of the pseudobulb; leaves are a decorative apple-green, and flowers are 2 to 3in. (5 to 8cm).

Aeranthes. This genus of about thirty species is native to Madagascar and adjacent islands. The unusual flowers – generally green – are either small or large.

Aerides. Sixty species form this epiphytic genus from Japan to India and Malaysia. Plants can grow 72in. (183cm) tall; they produce arching stems of small, handsome, and usually scented flowers.

Angraecum. Sometimes called Cyrtorchis, this genus of epiphytes is from Africa and bears star-shaped white blooms.

Anguloa. This terrestrial genus is comprised of ten species from the Andes. Large, colourful and fragrant flowers look somewhat like tulips. The plants are hard to grow but worth the trouble.

Ansellia. From tropical Africa, these spotted epiphytic or semi-epiphytic orchids display large and handsome flowers on medium- to large-sized plants. Only a few species are known.

Ascocentrum. This genus consists of nine species native to southern China, Java, and Borneo. They are brilliant orchids.

Barkeria. *See* Epidendrum.

Bifrenaria. From Panama and Brazil, this epiphytic genus consists of about twenty species. Most of these orchids have showy flowers and a solitary shiny green leaf. Flowers are produced in racemes rather than singly.

Bletia. These terrestrial species are found from Florida to Peru. The grass-like foliage is deciduous or nearly deciduous; the attractive flowers are small.

Bollea. A South American epiphytic genus with about six species. Handsome flowers are marked with blue; apple-green foliage is arranged in loose fans. This orchid is extremely desirable.

Brassavola. This epiphytic genus has about fifteen tropical American species; flowers are white or whitish green. *B. glauca* and *B. digbyana* have been hybridised with Cattleya species.

Brassia (Spider Orchids). About fifty species make up this epiphytic genus, native to south Florida and the West Indies to Mexico, Brazil, and Peru. The leafy plants have flowers (about fifty to a mature plant) with long sepals.

Calanthe. This genus has more than 150 terrestrial species distributed from South Africa to Asia and the Pacific Islands; in the West Indies and Central America it is a single species. Some Calanthes are evergreen; many are deciduous. Most of the cultivated hybrids bloom at Christmas.

Calopogon. These hardy North American terrestrials are common in Florida and the Bahamas. Leaves are grassy; the small flowers are quite handsome.

Catasetum. Epiphytic or occasionally semi-terrestrial, this genus has more than 100 species in the American tropics. The large and showy flowers are beautiful in some species, grotesque looking in others. Many of the species are deciduous; others hold their leaves until blooms appear.

Cattleya. The best-known genus of orchids. Most are epiphytic, but a few grow on rocks. The sixty-five species range from Mexico to Argentina and Peru. Plants have prominent pseudobulbs and one or two leaves. Cattleyas are the major orchids of commerce.

Chysis. A beautiful genus of epiphytic orchids with six or eight species throughout tropical America from Mexico to Peru. The leaves are thick and fleshy; flowers are showy.

Coelogyne. This genus has more than 120 epiphytic and terrestrial species distributed over the eastern hemisphere. Most of these plants prefer cool growing conditions; the flowers are showy, and plants have one or two leaves.

Comparettia. From Mexico to South America, this genus of epiphytic orchids has solitary leathery leaves and showy flowers. Not all species are attractive.

Coryanthes (Bucket orchids). This epiphytic genus has fifteen species ranging from British Honduras and Guatemala to Brazil and Peru. The plants have an intricate structure; more bizarre than beautiful, these orchids are rarely seen in cultivation.

Cycnoches (Swan orchids). This is a genus of about eleven species from tropical America. Usually deciduous, these epiphytic, sometimes terrestrial, orchids bear very fragrant and mammoth flowers. A plant looks like the neck of a swan.

Cymbidium. This is a genus of seventy epiphytic, semiepiphytic, and terrestrial species from the Asiatic tropics/subtropics. The leaves are broad, the flowers usually showy.

Cypripedium. This is the well-known Lady's slipper orchid. The genus contains about fifty species found in temperate and subtropical parts of the world. Plants are attractive with broad leaves and mostly showy flowers. There are about twelve species in the United States.

Dendrobium. This large genus has more than 1,500 species growing throughout the Asian tropics/subtropics to the Fiji Islands and Australia. Plants have bulbous or reed-like pseudobulbs. Some are evergreen; others are deciduous. There is wide variation of size, flower form, and plant structure. Some need heat; others prefer coolness.

Dendrochilum. *See* Platyclinis.

Diacrium (also called Caularthron). This epiphytic genus has four species, two of which are from the West Indies and Central America. All usually have hollow pseudobulbs. Flowers look a bit like those of the Epidendrums; plants are usually dwarf.

Doritis. This epiphytic genus is closely allied to Phalaenopsis. The flat-faced flowers are small but charming.

Epidendrum (Encyclia). This genus of more than 1,000 species ranges from North Carolina to Argentina. Most of the plants are epiphytic, although some grow in soil or on rocks. Plant form and flowers vary greatly. The two major groups of species are those with pseudobulbs and those with reed stem growth. Many of these orchids have been reclassified into the genera Encyclia, Barkeria, and Nanodes.

Eria. These epiphytic orchids are found mainly in India and Malaysia; there are more than 550 species. The plants are closely related to the genus Dendrobium. The flowers are usually small and not as showy as those of other orchids.

Galeandra. From tropical America, this genus is composed of about twenty-five terrestrial and epiphytic species. The leaves are grassy and folded.

Gastrochilus. A small genus of dwarf orchids, formerly called Saccolabium.

Gongora (Punch and Judy orchids). Twenty epiphytic species from tropical America make up this genus of incredible orchids that produce fragrant flower spikes from the base of the pseudobulbs.

Grammatophyllum. Native to Asia and the Pacific, this epiphytic genus includes eight species. Leaves are long and strap-shaped; spotted flowers last an incredibly long time. The plants are usually huge, to 120in. (305cm) in height.

Huntleya. This epiphytic genus has four species. Plants bear waxy flat-faced flowers that do not look like most orchid flowers.

Laelia. Here is a genus of mostly epiphytic orchids closely related to the genus Cattleya and found from Mexico to Argentina. The pseudobulbs are of various shapes, and the flowers resemble those of the Cattleyas but have narrower sepals and a less showy lip.

Leptotes. From Brazil and Paraguay, this epiphytic genus has four species. Plants are worth cultivating for their large blooms.

Lycaste. This terrestrial and epiphytic genus has about twenty-four species in tropical America and the West Indies. These popular plants are mainly deciduous; flowers are always showy and last six to eight weeks on the plants.

Macodes (Jewel orchids). This genus of seven species mainly from Indonesia and Malaysia has exquisitely coloured foliage. Plants require exacting care.

Masdevallia. About 300 orchids from tropical America compose this genus. Usually epiphytic, the brightly coloured, often oddly shaped, flowers are borne singly or sometimes on short spikes.

Miltonia (Pansy orchids). This important epiphytic genus, native to Brazil, Peru, and Costa Rica, includes about twenty species. Plants require differing conditions, depending on whether they are from high elevations or warm lowlands. The flat-faced flowers are lovely. Miltonia is used extensively for hybridising with Oncidium, Odontoglossum, and Brassia.

Mormodes (Flying birds orchids). This epiphytic genus of about twenty species is from the American tropics. Plants are deciduous or nearly so; flowers appear on leafless stalks.

Odontoglossum. This is a large epiphytic genus of 300 species from Mexico and South America, most from high elevations. Plants and flowers come in many shapes and sizes; some flowers are showy, but others are insignificant. This is a very important genus.

Oncidium (Dancing ladies). Most of the 750 epiphytic species are from South America and Central America. Blooms are small or large. Many species produce hundreds of small brown-and-yellow flowers.

Ornithocephalus. The thirty-five species of this mostly epiphytic genus are from Mexico and Brazil. The leaves are fan-like, the flowers small but attractive. Most species are dwarfs.

Ornithochilus. This epiphytic genus from the Himalayas and China is composed of two species. The pretty flowers are small; plants are rather dwarf-like.

Paphiopedilum (Lady's slipper orchid). This genus consists of about fifty Asiatic species that are mainly terrestrial. The flowers are waxy and almost artificial looking. Plants often mistakenly are called Cypripediums.

Pescatorea. This is a genus of about twelve epiphytic orchids from Costa Rica and Panama. The plants are medium-sized. The small, fleshy, and waxy flowers are exquisite looking.

Phaius. The thirty species in this genus range from East Africa to tropical Asia and the Pacific Islands. Generally, a terrestrial genus with but one epiphytic species.

Phalaenopsis (Moth orchids). Perhaps the most beautiful orchids belong to this epiphytic genus of some forty species which are found from Taiwan to India and the Philippines, New Guinea and Queensland, Australia. All species have leathery leaves and fine flowers. Plants have been extensively hybridised.

Phragmipedium. Often wrongly classified as Cypripedium or Selenipedium, plants of this genus of about twelve species from southern Mexico to Peru and Brazil have long, ribbon-like petals.

Platyclinis (Dendrochilum). Here is a genus of about 150 epiphytic orchids from Burma and Sumatra to New Guinea (many are also found in Borneo and the Philippines). Flowers are usually small

Pleurothallis. This genus of tropical American epiphytic orchids has almost 1,000 species. Some plants are large, others small; some flowers are desirable, those in other plants are not.

Pterostylis (Greenhoods). About seventy species of terrestrial orchids make up this genus. Most are from Australia; some are from New Zealand, New Guinea, and New Caledonia. The deciduous plants have small, usually green or greenish flowers with red-brown marks.

Renanthera. This is an epiphytic genus of showy plants from tropical Asia and some of the Pacific Islands. These orchids are famous for their brick-red colour.

Rhynchostylis. With only four species, this epiphytic genus (once included in the the genus Saccolabium) is very floriferous: a single plant may bear 200 highly scented flowers.

Rodriguezia. This genus of thirty dwarf epiphytic species grows from Costa Rica to Brazil and Peru. The dainty plants bear pendent scapes of colourful flowers.

Sarcochilus. This genus of epiphytic orchids contains about thirty species distributed over India, Malaysia, Australia, and the Pacific Islands. Some of these orchids have a tangle of roots rather than leaves. The flowers usually are handsome.

Schomburgkia. Closely related to Laelia, this genus extends from Mexico and the West Indies to South America. These orchids are epiphytics and may have two leaves and spindle-shaped pseudobulbs or larger hollow-shaped pseudobulbs with three or more leaves. In the wild, ant colonies often live in the hollow bulbs.

Selenipedium. This genus has four tropical American species. Most of these orchids are tall and reedy, with slipper-like flowers at the top. Most of the plants cultivated as Selenipedium are classified as Phragmipedium.

Spiranthes. This is a genus of about 300 species of American terrestrial orchids found in grasslands and woods.

Stenocoryne. From Brazil, this genus of twelve species is closely allied to Xylobium. The small flowers are usually bell-shaped and brilliantly coloured.

Stenoglottis. These terrestrial orchids are from South Africa. The tuberous roots produce a rosette of leaves; the flowers are small but attractive. Plants grow and bloom for four or five months and then rest for a few months before repeating the cycle.

Telipogon. Difficult to grow in cultivation but worth a try, these generally dwarf epiphytes from Costa Rica and Peru bear gorgeous triangular-shaped flowers.

Trichocentrum. This genus of eighteen species is from tropical America. Plants are mostly dwarf, with small but appealing flowers.

Trichoceros. This genus of epiphytes has six species rarely cultivated. Plants are native to Colombia, Peru, and Bolivia.

Trichoglottis. These vine-like plants from Asia and Indonesia bear pretty flowers. The genus has thirty-five epiphytic species.

Trichopilia. With about thirty species, this epiphytic genus is native to Mexico, Central America and Colombia. The large flowers hug the rim of their container.

Vanda. This epiphytic genus of seventy species extends from China and the Himalayas to New Guinea and northern Australia. Plants have strap-shaped or cylindrical leaves and long-lasting flat-faced flowers. Hundreds of hybrids have been produced.

Warscewiczella. *See* Zygopetalum.

Xylobium. From tropical America, this genus of twenty species is usually epiphytic but sometimes terrestrial. Flowers are usually small and pale in colour.

Zygopetalum. This is an epiphytic genus of twenty species from tropical and Central America. The very fragrant flowers are a combination of spots and stripes of blue, green, and brown.

Orchids for the Beginner

These orchids are generally easy to grow under average conditions.

Bletia purpurea
Brassavola cucullata
B. nodosa
Brassia caudata
B. gireoudiana
B. maculata
Calanthe rosea
C. vestita
Cattleya citrina
C. forbesii
Dendrobium aggregatum
D. nobile
D. pierardii
D. thyrsiflorum

Epidendrum atropurpureum
E. fragrans
E. o'brienianum
Lycaste aromatica
L. deppei
L. skinneri
Oncidium ampliatum
O. sarcodes
Phaius grandifolius
Stanhopea oculata
S. wardii
Trichopilia elegans
T. suavis
T. tortilis

~ APPENDIX 4 ~
Orchid Types

These are the four basic orchid flowering types.

Single-flowered (one flower to a stem, but sometimes two or more stems in bloom at the same time)

Cattleya citrina
Laelia pumila
Lycaste aromatica
L. deppei
L. gigantea
L. skinneri
Miltonia spectabilis
Pleione maculata

Cluster Flowering

Dendrobium chrysotoxum
D. thyrsiflorum
Epidendrum o'brienianum
Laelia superbiens
Phaius grandifolius

Spray Orchids

Calanthe vestita
Dendrobium aggregatum
E. stamfordianum
Oncidium ampliatum
O. ornithorynchum
O. sarcodes
O. wentworthianum

Pendent Orchids

Aerides crassifolium
A. odoratum
Brassia maculata
Dendrobium pierardii
D. superbum

~ APPENDIX 5 ~
Plant Location

This is a general guide to the light requirements of popular orchid types.

Warm Location

Aerides odoratum
Brassia maculata
Dendrobium chrysotoxum
Stanhopea oculata
S. wardii

Full Sun

Aerides odoratum
Brassavola cucullata
B. digbyana
B. nodosa
Brassia maculata
Dendrobium aggregatum
D. chrysotoxum
Epidendrum atropurpureum
E. prismatocarpum
Laelia superbiens
Oncidium ampliatum

Cold Location

Cattleya citrina
Epidendrum vitellinum
Laelia superbiens
Miltonia vexillaria
Pleione maculata

Shaded Window

Cypripedium insigne
Epidendrum vitellinum
Stanhopea oculata
S. wardii

～ APPENDIX 6 ～
Orchid Suppliers

The inclusion of an orchid mail order source does not constitute an endorsement for that company. Nor are all companies listed here. Addresses change and some companies go out of business, so write first or telephone.

INTERNATIONAL

International movement of all plant materials requires CITES except seedlings in vitro (flasks).

The Bangkrabue Nursery
174 Ruam Chit Lane
Amnuai Songkhram Road
P.O. Box 3-150
Bangkok 3, Thailand 10 300
Orchids of Thailand

Caribe Orchid Growers
P.O. Box 26
Carolina, Puerto Rico 00628
Species

Green Orchids Company
P.O. Box 7-587
Taipei, Taiwan, R.O.C.
Cattleyas

Kabukiran Orchids
81 Maginoo Street
P.O. Box 7744 ADC
Quezon City, Philippines
Philippine orchids

E.G. Kamm
Valle de Angeles, F.M.
Honduras
Species

Marcel Lecoufle
5 rue de Paris
94470 Boissy-st. Leger
France

Nurseryman's Haven
Kalimpong 734301
India
Indo-Burmese, Himalayan orchids

Sukhakul Nursery
15 Klahom Lane
P.O. Box 3-97
Bangkok 3
Thailand
Thai orchid species; free list

T. Orchids
77/3 Chaengwattana Road
Pak-kred Nonthaburi, Thailand
P.O. Box 21-19
Bangkok
Thailand
Dendrobiums, Vandas; catalogue, price list $5

Vacherot & Lecoufle
30 rue de Valenton, BP 8
94470 Boissy-St. Leger
France
All genera

UNITED KINGDOM

The Royal Horticultural Society holds the annual London Orchid Show every March at the Royal Horticultural Society Hall, Vincent Square, Westminster, London.

Burnham Nurseries and Orchid Paradise
Forches Cross
Newton Abbot
Devon
TQ12 6PZ

Deva Orchids
Littlebrook Farm
Sryt Isa
Pen-y-ffordd
Chester
CH4 0JY

Equatorial Plant Company
7 Gray Lane
Barnard Castle
Co Durham
DL12 8PD

Greenaway Orchids
Rookery Farm
Puxton
Near Weston-super-Mare
Avon
BS24 6TL

Laurence Hobbs Orchids Ltd
Bailiffs Cottage Nurseries
Hophurst Lane
Crawley Down
West Sussex RH10 4LN

Ivens Orchids
'Great Barn Dell'
St Albans Road
Sandridge
St Albans
Hertfordshire
AL4 9LB

A J Keeling & Sons
Grange Nurseries
North View Road
Westgate Hill
Bradford
West Yorkshire
BO4 6NS

McBean's Orchids
Cooksbridge
Lewes
East Sussex
BN8 4PR

Mansell & Hatcher Ltd
Cragg Wood Nurseries
Woodlands Drive
Rawdon
Leeds
LS19 6LQ

Only Phalaenopsis
20 Saturn Close
Leighton Buzzard
Bedfordshire
LU7 8UU

Phoenix Orchids
Pennine House
50 Pinnar Lane
Southowram
Halifax
HX3 9QT

Plested Orchids
38 Florence Road
College Town
Sandhurst
Berkshire
GU47 0QD

Ratcliffe Orchids Ltd
Pitcot Lane
Owslebury
Winchester
SO21 1LR

Royden Orchids
Perks Lane
Prestwood
Great Missenden
Buckinghamshire
HP16 0JD

David Stead Orchids
Langley Farm
Westgate Lane
Lofthouse
Wakefield
WF3 3PA

Stonehurst Nurseries
Ardingly
Sussex
RH17 6TN

Woodstock Orchids & Automation Division
Woodstock House
50 Pound Hill
Great Brickhill
Nr Milton Keynes
MK17 9AS

UNITED STATES

Alberts & Merkel Bros., Inc.
2210 South Federal Highway
Boynton Beach FL 33435

The Angraecum House,
P.O. Box 976
Grass Valley CA 95945
Madagascan and other African species

Arm-Roy, 3376 Foothill Road
P.O. Box 385
Carpenteria CA 93013
Botanicals

Bates Orchids, Inc.
7911 U.S. Highway 301
Ellenton FL 33532-3599
Botanicals

Blueberry Hill Orchids
12 Charles Street
Lexington MA 02173
Phalaenopsis

Bo-Mar Orchids
P.O. Box 6713
San Bernardino CA 92412
Cattleyas

Carter & Holmes, Inc.
1 Old Mendenhall Road
P.O. Box 608
Newberry SC 29108
All types of orchids

La Casa Verde,
35601 SW 192nd Avenue,
Homestead FL 33034
All types of orchids

Chester Hills Orchids
962 Catfish Lane
Pottstown PA 19464
Phalaenopsis

Chula Orchids
230 Chula Vista Street
Chula Vista CA 92010
Botanicals

Clark Day Orchids
1911 South Bloomfield
Cerritos CA 90701
Odontoglossums

John Ewing Orchids
P.O. Box 384
Aptos CA 95003
Phalaenopsis

Exotics Hawaii Limited
1344 Hoakoa Place
Honolulu HI 96821
Cattleyas, Dendrobiums, Vandas, Oncidiums

E-Z Orchids
Box 209
Berwyn PA 19312
Phalaenopsis, Cattleyas

Fordyce Orchids
7259 Tina Place
Dublin CA 94568
Miniature Cattleyas

Fort Caroline Orchids
13142 Fort Caroline Road
Jacksonville FL 32225
Botanicals, Brassias

Hausermann Orchids
2 N 134 Addison Road
Villa Park IL 60181
Large selection

Huan Bui Orchids, Inc.
6900 SW 102nd Avenue
Miami FL 33173
Seedlings

Islander Delights Orchids
14568 Twin Peaks Road
Poway CA 92064
Oncidiums, Dendrobiums, Vandas; free list

J & L Orchids
4996 NE Fourth Avenue
Boca Raton FL 33430
Miniature Cattleyas, Oncidiums

Jemmco Flowers
Box 23
St. George SC 29477

Kaoru Oka Orchids
1346 Wilhelmina Rise
Honolulu HI 96816
Cattleyas

Kensington Orchids, Inc.
3301 Plyers Mill Road
Kensington MD 20795
Cattleyas,botanicals

Arnold J. Klemm, Grower
2 E. Algonquin Road
Arlington Heights IL 60005
Phalaenopsis

Krull-Smith Orchids
Ponkan Road, Route 3
Box 18A
Apopka FL 32703
Cattleyas, Phalaenopsis

Laurel Orchids
18205 SW 157th Avenue
Miami FL 33187
Botanicals, seedlings

Lines Orchids
1823 Taft Highway
Signal Mountain TN 37377
Seedlings; Cattleyas

Rod McLellan Co.
1450 El Camino Real
San Francisco CA 94080
Oncidiums, Cattleyas; catalogue $0.50

Madcap Orchids
Route 29, Box 391-UU
Fort Myers FL 33905

Maka Koa Corporation
Box 411
Haleiwa HI 96712
Cattleyas

Maxwell Company
P.O. Box 13141
Fresno CA 93794

Merryl's
Division of Miah, Inc.
6660 Busch Boulevard
Columbus OH 43229
Miniatures

Mobile Bay Orchids
Route 1, Box 166-D
Mobile AL 36605
Various

Oak Hill Gardens
P.O. Box 25
Dundee IL 60118
Botanicals

The Orchid Center
Highway 17, Box 16
Arcadia FL 33821

The Orchid House
1699 Sage Avenue
Los Osos CA 93402
Phalaenopsis

Orchid Species Specialties
P.O. Box 1003
Arcadia CA 91006
Species

Orchid World International
11295 SW 93rd Street
Miami FL 33176
Cattleyas, Oncidiums, others

Orchidland
920 Homer Road
Woodstock GA 30188
Phalaenopsis

Orchids Bountful
826 West 3800 South
Bountiful UT 84010
Species

Orchids Ltd.
407 E. Carson Street
Carson CA 90745
All types of orchids

Owens Orchids
P.O. Box 365
Pisgah Forest NC 28768
Miniature and small Cattleyas

Paradise of Orchids
1608 Waterline Road
Bradenton FL 34202
Vandaceous orchids

Pearl Harbor Orchids
99-007 Kealakaha Drive
Aiea HI 96701

Quality Orchids
P.O. Box 4472
Hialeah FL 33014
Send for list

R.F. Orchids
28100 SW 182nd Avenue
Homestead FL 33030
Vandas

J.R. Rands Orchids
15322 Mullholland Drive
Los Angeles CA 90077
Cattleyas, botanicals

Joseph R. Redlinger Orchids
9236 SW 57th Avenue
Miami FL 33156
Cattleyas

Ridgeway Orchid Gardens
2467 Ridgeway Drive
National City CA 92050
Phalaenopsis

Seagulls Landing Orchids
P.O. Box 388
Glen Head NY 11545
Miniature Cattleyas

Stewart Orchids, Inc.
1212 E. Las Tunas Drive
P.O. Box 307
San Gabriel CA 91778
Cattleyas, including miniatures

Sin-An Nursery
58 Kirklees Road
Pittsford NY 14534
Phalaenopsis, Cattleyas

Sunswept Laboratories
P.O. Box 1913
Studio City CA 91604
Phalaenopsis

Ken West Orchids
P.O. Box 1332
Pahoa HI 96778

Wilk Orchid Specialties
P.O. Box 1177
Kaneohe HI 96744
Assorted orchids

Yamamoto Dendrobiums Hawaii
P.O. Box 1003
Arcadia CA 91006
Botanicals

Zuma Canyon Orchids, Inc.
5949 Bonsall Drive
Malibu CA 90265
Phalaenopsis

~ APPENDIX 7 ~
Equipment Suppliers and Book Dealers

UNITED KINGDOM

Ratcliffe Orchids Ltd.
Owslebury, Winchester SO21 1LR
Orchid books (old and new) and orchid sundries

C. H. Whitehouse Ltd.
Buckhurst Works
Frant, Sussex TN3 9BN
All-cedar orchid houses, ventilation and heating equipment

UNITED STATES

Clarel Laboratories, Inc.
513 Grove
Deerfield IL 60015
Orchid food

Day's
4725 NW 36th Avenue
Miami FL 33142
Tier plant benches

Environmental Concepts
710 NW 57th Street
Fort Lauderdale FL 33309
Light-intensity meters

Idle Hours Orchids
905 SW Coconut Drive
Fort Lauderdale FL 33315
Servo orchid potting mix

Indoor Gardening Supplies
P.O. Box 40567 AO
Detroit MI 48240
Plant stands, lamps, accessories;

Keiki Grow, Dr. James D. Brasch
Box 354, McMaster University
Hamilton, Ontario L85 1C0 Canada
Plant hormones

B.D. Lynn
1438 West Valerio Street
Santa Barbara CA 93101
Orchids in gold (jewellery)

McQuerry Orchid Books
Mary Noble McQuerry
5700 West Salerno Road
Jacksonville FL 32244
Rare, old, and new books

Ofiduca International, Inc.
P.O. Box 161302
Miami FL 33116
Potting mediums

Orchid Art Gallery
1765 Victory Boulevard
Staten Island NY 10314
Indoor greenhouses

Orchid Lovers' Sales Directory & Guide to Regional Sources
P.O. Box 17125
Rochester NY 14617
Regional guidebook to orchid societies; write for price

Pacific Coast Greenhouse Manufacturing Co.
8360 Industrial Avenue
Cotati CA 94928
Humidifiers; free brochures and price list

Spiral Filtration, Inc.
747 North Twin Oaks Valley Road.
San Marco CA 92069
Water-purification system

Tropical Plant Products, Inc.
P.O. Box 7754
Orlando FL 32854
*Tree fern products, potting mediums,
fertilisers, wire goods*

Yonah Manufacturing Co.
P.O. Box 280 AO
Cornelia GA 30531
Shade cloth; free informational kit

~ APPENDIX 8 ~
Orchid Societies

Membership in any society listed here includes the society's worth-while publication.

AUSTRALIA
Australian Orchid Review
Sydney Mail Exchange
Australia 2012
Published quarterly

South Africa
M. Byren
South African Orchid Council
P.O. Box 81
Constantia
7848 South Africa

UNITED KINGDOM

The Birmingham & Midland Society
26 Halesowen Road
Halesowen
West Midlands
B62 9AA
Contact: J E E Hodgkins

The Bournemouth Orchid Society
11 Lacon Close
Bitterne Park
Southampton
SO18 1JA
Contact: Mrs Ann Slade

The Bristol and West of England Orchid Society
'Vron'
Bath Road
Leonard Stanley
Stonehouse
Gloucestershire
GL10 3LR
Contact: Mr John Hale

British Odontoglossum Alliance
Ouchthorpe Farm
Ouchthorpe Lane
Outwood
Wakefield
West Yorkshire
WF1 3HS
Contact: John Gay

The British Orchid Growers' Association
Plested Orchids
38 Florence Road
College Town
Sandhurst
Berkshire
GU47 0QD
Contact: Mrs Janet Plested (BOGA Secretary)

British Paphiopedilum Society
c/o Ratcliffe Orchids Ltd.
Owslebury, Winchester SO21 1LR

Cambridge Orchid Society
'Syringa'
63 Highfields Road
Caldecote
Cambridgeshire
CB3 7NX
Contact: Mrs Brenda Morley

The Central Orchid Society
15 Orwell Close
Norton
Stourbridge
DY8 3JS
Contact: Mrs Helen J Miller

The Cheltenham and District Orchid Society
15 Lapwing Close
Northway
Tewkesbury
Gloucestershire
GL20 8TN
Contact: Mr Rod Wells, Hon.
Secretary

The Cheshire and North Wales Orchid Society
31 Windermere Road
Birkenhead
Merseyside
L43 9SJ
Contact: Harold Kitchen

The Cotswold Amateur Orchid Society
Barn Cottage
Chapel Lane
Enstone
Chipping Norton
Oxon
OX7 4NB
Contact: Dr Janet Newson

The Cumbria Orchid Society
Stanegate
Newcastle Road
Brampton
Cumbria
CA8 1ES
Contact: Mr E Rowntree

The Devon Orchid Society
Willand Post Office
Willand Old Village
Cullompton
Devon
EX15 2RJ
Contact: Mrs Sue Lane

The East Anglia Orchid Society
48 Procter Road
Sprowston
Norwich
NR6 7PQ
Contact: Jack H Butcher

The East Midlands Orchid Society
25 Burnside Grove
Tollerton
Nottingham
NG12 4ET
Contact: A L Deakin

The Eric Young Orchid Foundation
Victoria Village
Trinity
Jersey
Channel Islands
JE3 5HH

Fenland Orchid Society
8 Sutton Meadows
Leverington
Wisbech
PE13 5ED
Contact: Mr Bob Green

Glasgow Botanic Garden
Great Wester Road
Glasgow
G12 0UE
Contact: David Menzies

Harrogate Orchid Society
32 Stainburn Road
Leeds
LS17 6NN
Contact:Dr Martin Brice

Hinckley & District Orchid Society
79 Hereford Close
Barwell
Leicester
LE9 8HU
Contact: Mr Keith Bates

The Isle of Wight Orchid Society
65 St David's Road
East Cowes
Isle of Wight
PO32 6EF
Contact: Mr J Lashmar, (Hon. Secretary)

The Lea Valley Orchid Society
49 Malcolm Crescent
Hendon
London
NW4 4PL
Contact: Michael Potter

Mid Sussex Orchid Society
9 Harlands Close
Haywards Heath
West Sussex
RH16 1PS
Contact: Dr Maria Firth

North Bucks Orchid Society
50 Drayton Road
Bletchley
Milton Keynes
Buckinghamshire
MK2 2ES
Contact: Mrs G Banham

The North East of England Orchid Society
57 Bede Burn View
Jarrow
Tyne & Wear
NE32 5PQ
Contact: W McMullen

The North of England Orchid Society
Ouchthorpe Farm
Ouchthorpe Lane
Outwood
Wakefield
WF1 3HS
Contact: Mr J Gay

North Hampshire Orchid Society
18 Gannet Close
Basingstoke
Hampshire
RG22 5QN
Contact: Mrs Rose Henwood

Northern Ireland Orchid Society
76 Ravenhill
Belfast
BT6 0DG
Contact: Mrs l McCartan

The North Staffordshire Orchid Society
The Bungalow
Peacock Lane
Hanchurch
Stoke-on-Trent
ST4 8RZ

The Orchid Society of Great Britain
Athelney
145 Binscombe Village
Godalming
Surrey
GU7 3QL
Contact: Mrs Betty Arnold

The Royal Botanic Gardens
Kew
Richmond
Surrey
TW9 3AB
Contact: Sandra Bell

The Royal Horticultural Society
The R H S Garden
Wisley
Woking
Surrey
GU23 6QB
Contact: Mrs Joyce Stewart

The Scottish Orchid Society
164 Eskhill
Peniculk
Mid-Lothian
EH26 8DQ
Contact: Mr Alan F E Benson

Aberdeen Branch
51 Binghill Road West
Aberdeen
AB1 7SS
Contact: Noel Kent

Dundee Branch
49 Tweed Crescent
Dundee
DD2 4DG
Contact: Mrs Margaret Morris

Edinburgh Branch
39 Liberton Drive
Edinburgh
EH16 6NL
Contact: Mrs Muriel Ridout

Glasgow Branch
27 Dumgoyne Drive
Bearsden
Glasgow
G6 13AP
Contact: Mrs Dorothea Macdonald

Perth Branch
Trynmuir
Drum Road
Cupar
Fife
KY15 5RJ
Contact: Mr Joe Dobson

Sheffield & District Orchid Society
Whitecroft
170 Watt Lane
Sheffield
S10 5QN
Contact: J L Williams

The Solihull and District Orchid Society
61 Stanwell Lea
Middleton Cheney
Banbury
OX17 2RF
Contact: Mr P White

The Somerset Orchid Society
'Sunrays'
Newtown
West Pennard
Glastonbury
Somerset
BA6 8NL
Contact: Mrs B House

The Southern Counties Orchid Society
50 Golden Avenue
East Preston
West Sussex
BN16 1QX
Contact: Mrs J B Smith

The South Orchid Society
33 Albany Road
Capel-le-Ferne
Folkstone
Kent
CT18 7LA
Contact: Mrs J Hooker

South Wales Orchid Society
7 Wimmerfield Avenue
Swansea
West Glamorgan
SA2 7BT
Contact: Mr B Hendy

South West Orchid Society
Lowenva Ham
Creech St Michael
Taunton
Somerset
TA3 5NY
Contact: Mrs B Holdaway

Suffolk Orchid Society
Green Tyles
Nettlestead
Ipswich
Suffolk
IP8 4QS
Contact: Mrs Monica McLaren

Sussex Orchid Group
103 North Road
Three Bridges
Crawley
West Sussex
RH10 1SQ
Contact: Mrs V Micklewright

The Thames Valley Orchid Society
White's Farm House
Letcombe Bassett
Wantage
Oxon
OX12 9LW

The Wessex Orchid Society
Helvellyn
4 Southampton Road
Fareham
Hampshire
PO16 7DY
Contact: Mrs Stella Allison

The West Cornwall Orchid Society
St Martin's Villa
13 Pendraves Road
Camborne
Cornwall
TR14 7QB
Contact: Mrs K Lindsay

The Wiltshire Orchid Society
4a The Picquet
Bratton
Westbury
Wiltshire
BA13 4RU
Contact: Mrs J Hornsey

The Worcestershire Orchid Society
23 The Birches
Stourport on Severn
Worcestershire
DY13 9NW
Contact: Mrs Alison Caldwell

Mid Wales Orchid Society
The Old Cricket
Broadheath
Presteigne
Powys
LD8 2HG
Contact: Mrs L Rees-Roberts

UNITED STATES

The American Orchid Society
6000 South Olive Street
West Palm Beach FL 33405

The Orchid Digest Corporation
c/o Mrs. Norman H. Atkinson
P.O. Box 916
Carmichael CA 95609-0916

South Florida Orchid Society
13300 SW 111th Avenue
Miami FL 33176

Glossary

AERIAL ROOTS – roots growing outside the potting mix or hanging free in the air
ANTHER – the part of the *stamen* that contains *pollen*
ASEXUAL – propagation by *division* and *meristem*
AXIL – the upper angle between a stem or branch and a leaf

BACKBULB – the older *pseudobulb* behind the growing lead
BIFOLIATE – having two leaves
BIGENERIC – involving two *genera* in the parentage of a plant
BISEXUAL – two-sexed; flowers possess both *stamens* and *pistils*
BOTANICAL – refers to *species* not grown for cut flowers
BRACT – a leaf-like *sheath* near the base of the flower stem
BULB – plant structure used for storage; generally includes *corms*, *rhizomes* and *tubers* as well as true bulbs
BULBOUS – having the shape and character of a bulb

CALYX – outer circle of floral parts, usually green
CHLOROTIC – excessive yellowing from the breaking down of chlorophyll
CHROMOSOMES – structures within the cell nucleus that carry the *genes*
CLONE – a sexually produced, seed-grown individual and all its subsequent asexual (vegetative) propagations
COLUMN – the central body of the orchid flower, formed by the union of the *stamens* and *pistil*
COMPOST – decomposed vegetable matter
CULTIVAR – plant form originating in cultivation
CUTTING – vegetable plant part capable of producing an identical plant

DECIDUOUS – describes plants that lose leaves at maturity in certain seasons
DIPLOID – orchid with the normal number of chromosomes
DIVISION – the means by which a single *cultivar* is divided into two or more plants
DORMANCY – resting; a period of inactivity when plants grow less or not at all
DORSAL – pertaining to the back or outer surface

EPIPHYTE – a plant that grows on another plant, but is not a *parasite* because it obtains its nourishment from the air
EYE – the bud of a growth
FAMILY – a group of related *genera*
FORCE – to make a plant grow or bloom ahead of its natural season

GENE – the unit of inheritance, located at a specific site on a chromosome
GENERA – group of plants. The plural of *genus*

GENETICS – the study of heredity and variation

GENUS – a subdivision of a family, consisting of one or more *species* that show similar characteristics and appear to have a common ancestry

GERMINATION – the process of seed sprouting

GREX – the named cross between two different orchids

HABITAT – the locality in which a plant normally grows

HIRSUTE – pubescent, the hairs being coarse and stiff

HYBRID – the offspring resulting from the cross between two different *species* or *genera*

INDIGENOUS – native; not introduced

INFLORESCENCE – the flowering part of a plant

INTERGENERIC – between or among two or more *genera*

INTERNODE – the part of stem between two *nodes*

KEIKI – a plantlet produced as an offset or offshoot from another plant; a Hawaiian term used by orchidists

LABELLUM – the *lip*, or modified *petal*, or an orchid flower

LANCEOLATE – shaped like a lance

LATERAL – of or pertaining to the side of an organ

LEAD – a new vegetative growth

LEAFLET – a segment of a compound leaf

LEAF MOULD – decayed or decomposed leaves, useful in potting mixes

LINEAR – long and narrow, with parallel margins

LIP – the *labellum*, usually quite different from the other two *petals*

LITHOPHYTE – a plant that grows on rocks

MERICLONE – a plant produced by *meristem* culture

MERISTEM – the quickly developing plant tissue at the point of growth

MERISTEM CULTURE – clonal propagation of plants

MONOPODIAL – growing only from the apex of the plant

MUTATION – a departure from the parent type; a *sport*

NATURAL HYBRID – a *hybrid* produced by change in the wild

NODE – a joint on a stem where a bud or leaf is attached

NOMENCLATURE – a system of names or naming

OFFSET – a plantlet that may form at the base of an orchid or on the stem, *pseudobulb*

PARASITE – a plant that lives on and derives part or all of its nourishment from another plant

PETAL – one of the three inner segments of an orchid flower, not modified to form the *lip*

PETIOLE – supporting stalk of a leaf

PINNATE – leaf form, like a feather, with sections arranged along the sides of the leaf stalk

PISTIL – the seed-bearing organ of a flower, consisting of the *stigma, style* and *ovary*

PLICATE – pleated or folded like a fan

POLLEN – the fertilising grains borne by the *anther*

POLLINATION – the transfer of *pollen* from the *anther* to the *stigma*

POLYPLOID – containing one or more additional sets of *chromosomes* beyond the normal *diploid* number

POTBOUND – condition of a plant when a mat of roots fills the container

PROTOCORM – a *tuber*-like structure formed in the early stages of a plant's development

PSEUDOBULB – the thickened portion of a stem, but not a true *bulb*

QUADRIGENERIC – pertaining to four *genera*

RACEME – a simple *inflorescence* of stalked flowers

RHIZOME – a root-bearing horizontal stem that, in orchids, usually lies on or just beneath the ground surface

ROSETTE – a cluster of leaves arranged around a short stem

SACCATE – pouched or bag-like

SCANDENT – sprawling

SCAPE – a flower stalk without leaves, arising directly from the ground

SELF-POLLINATION – the *pollination* of a flower by its own *pollen*

SEMITERETE – semicircular in cross section; semicylindrical

SEPAL – one of the three outer segments of an orchid flower

SHEATH – a tubular envelope protecting the developing buds or stems

SPECIES – a group of plants sharing one or more common characteristics

SPHAGNUM MOSS – bog material dried and used alone as a planting medium or in a mixture

SPIKE – a flower stem

SPORT – a deviation from the usual form; a *mutation*

SPUR – a hollow, tubular extension of the *lip*

STAMEN – the male organ of a flower, bearing the *pollen*

STIGMA – the part of the pistil that is receptive to the *pollen*

STOLON – creeping, horizontal stem usually producing a new plant at the tip

STYLE – the part of the *pistil* bearing the *stigma*

SUCCULENT – type of plant that stores moisture in stems or leaves

SYMBIOSIS – the close association of dissimilar organisms, with benefits to both

SYMPODIAL – form of growth in which each new shoot, arising from the *rhizome* of previous growth, is a complete plant in itself

TAXONOMIST – scientific specialist concerned with organism classification and names

TERETE – circular in cross section; cylindrical

TERRESTRIAL – growing in or on the ground

TETRAPLOID – plant cells with four times the normal number of *chromosomes*, compared to common *species* having a *diploid* number of *chromosomes*

TRANSPIRATION – loss of water from the plant tissue by evaporation

TRIBE – a group of related *genera*, e.g.

TRIGENERIC – pertaining to three *genera*

TUBER – a thickened, normally underground stem

UMBEL – flat or ball-shaped flower cluster

UNIFOLIATE – having one leaf

UNILATERIAL – arranged only on one side

UNISEXUAL – having flowers of one sex only

VANDACEOUS – refers to Vanda *genus* and to other plants that similarly have a *monopodial* type of growth

VEGETATIVE PROPAGATION – the increasing of a particular plant by *division*, *offset*, *keiki*, etc.

VELAMEN – outer coating of root

VIRUS – an infectious agent that increases in living cells, causing disease

Bibliography

Some of the books listed herein are out of print but can be secured through antiquarian book dealers or found in libraries.

Ames, Blanche, *Drawings of Florida Orchids*, 2nd ed, explanatory notes by Oakes Ames, Botanical Museum of Harvard University, 1959.
— and Donovan S. Correll, *Orchids of Guatemala*, Field Museum of Natural History, Chicago, 1952-1953. (Fieldiana: *Botany*, vol. 26, nos. 1 and 2.) Supplement by Correll, 2 vols., 1966.

Blowers, John, *Pictorial Orchid Growing.* John W. Blowers, 96 Marion Crescent, Maidstone, Kent 1966.

Cady, Leo and T. Rotherham. *Australian Orchids in Colour,* Sydney: Reed, 1970.
Chittenden, Fred J., *Dictionary of Gardening.* 4 vols., Clarendon Press, 1951, 1956, 1965.
Correll, Donovan S., *Native Orchids of North America, North of Mexico,* Ronald Press, New York, 1950.
Craighead, Frank S., *Orchids and Other Air Plants of the Everglades National Park,* University of Miami Press, 1963.

Dodson, Calaway H. and Robert J. Gillespie, *The History of the Orchid,* Mid-America Orchid Congress, Nashville, 1967.
Dunsterville, G.C.K., *Introduction to the World of Orchids,* Doubleday, 1964

Fennell, T. A., Jr., *Orchids for Home and Garden,* Rinehart, 1956; rev. ed., 1959.

Garrard, Jeanne, *Growing Orchids for Pleasure,* Barnes, 1966.
Ghose, B. N., *Beautiful Indian Orchids,* Ghose, India, 1959; 2nd ed., 1969.
Graf, Alfred Byrd, *Exotica 3: Pictorial Cyclopedia of Exotic Plants,* NJ. Rutherford, Roehrs, 1963.
Grubb, Roy and Ann Grubb, *Selected Orchidaceous Plants. Parts 1-3,* Roy and Ann Grubb, 62 Chaldon Common Rd., Caterham, Surrey, England, 1961-1963. Drawn and hand printed by the authors.

Harvard University Botanical Museum Leaflets, by subscription or available separately from the American Orchid Society, 6000 South Olive St., West Palm Beach, FL 33405.
Hawkes, Alex D. *Encyclopedia of Cultivated Orchids,* Faber & Faber, 1965.
— *Orchids: Their Botany and Culture,* Harper & Row, 1961.

Kramer, Jack. *Growing Orchids at Your Windows,* Van Nostrand, 1963.
—*The World Wildlife Fund Book of Orchids.* Abbeville, 1989.

Moulen, Fred, *Orchids in Australia* Australia Edita, Sydney, 1958.

Noble, Mary, *You Can Grow Cattleya Orchids*. Mary Noble, 3003 Riverside Ave., Jacksonville, FL, 1968.

Northen, Rebecca Tyson, *Orchids as House Plants*, 2nd rev. ed, New York, 1955, 1976.

Oca, Rafael Montes de, *Hummingbirds and Orchids of Mexico*. Fournier, Mexico City, 1963.

Richter, Walter, *The Orchid World*, New York, 1965, revised and translated from the 1958 edition.

Sander, David, *Orchids and Their Cultivation*, rev. ed, Blandford, 1962.

Sander, Fred, *Reichenbachia: Orchids Illustrated and Described*. 4 vols, London, 1888-1894.

Sander & Sons, *Sander's Orchid Guide*, rev. ed., Sanders, St. Albans, England, 1927.
— *Complete List of Orchid Hybrids*. Sanders, St. Albans, England, 1946. Addenda, 3 vols., 1946-1948, 1949-1951, 1952-1954.
— *One-Table List of Orchid Hybrids, 1946-1960*, 2 vols, Sanders, St. Albans, England, Sanders, 1961. Addenda, 1963, 1966.
— *Sander's List of Orchid Hybrids*, Royal Horticultural Society. Addenda, 1961-1970, 1971-1975, 1976-1980. Also available from the American Orchid Society, 6000 South Olive Street, West Palm Beach FL 33405.

Schelpe, E.A.C.L.E., *An Introduction to the South African Orchids*, Macdonald, 1966.

Schweinfurth, Charles, *Orchids of Peru*, 4 vols. Field Museum of Natural History, Chicago, 1958-1961. (Fieldiana: *Botany*, vol. 30, nos. 1-4.).

Veitch, James & Sons. *A Manual of Orchidaceous Plants*, 4 vols, reprint, Ashler, Amsterdam, 1963.

Watkins, John V., *ABCs of Orchid Growing*, 3rd ed., Prentice-Hall, 1956.

White, E. A., *American Orchid Culture*, rev. ed. De la Mare, New York, 1942.

Williams, John G. and Andrew E., *Field Guide to Orchids of North America*, Universe Books, New York, 1983.

Williams, Louis O., *The Orchidaceae of Mexico*. Escuela Agricola Panamericana, Tegucigalpa, Honduras, 1952. (*Cieba*, vol. 2, in 4 parts.)

Withner, Carl L., *The Orchids: A Scientific Survey*. Ronald, New York, 1959.

Photographic Credits

Andrew Addkison: 14, 27, 28, 29, 30, 31, 32, 34, 44, 46, 60, 62, 63, 64, 65, 66, 100, 102, 104, 106, 108, 109, 111, 112, 116, 119, 120, 121, 122, 129, 131, 133, 136, 138, 139, 145, 147, 149, 156, 160, 162, 165, 167, 168, 174, 175

Author: 17, 24, 25, 41, 42, 56, 57, 68, 69, 70, 71, 72, 73, 74, 97, 100, 101, 102, 103, 104, 106, 107, 108, 110, 111, 112, 118, 119, 120, 122, 123, 124, 125, 126, 127, 128, 129, 130, 133, 135, 140, 141, 144, 147, 150, 151, 156, 158, 159, 160, 161, 162, 163, 164, 166, 167, 170, 171, 172

Cal Orchids: 102, 105, 116, 155

Carol Carlson: 77, 78, 79, 81, 82, 83

Tom Clark: 67, 68

Jeff Corder: 47, 50, 51, 165

Roy Crafton: 33

Geoffrey Hands: 55, 130, 142, 143

Paul Hutchinson: 40, 41, 42

Jem Orchids: 96, 105, 121, 134, 136, 152

Longwood Gardens: 27

Mrs. Fordyce Marsh: 39, 43, 44, 45, 47, 48, 49, 50, 52, 53, 54, 59, 99, 121, 123, 171, frontispiece, endpapers

Adrian Martinez: 84, 85

Hans Meyer: 99, 118

Hermann Pigors: 40, 42, 52, 55, 57, 58, 59, 124, 126, 137, 138, 151

William Shaban: 69, 96, 97, 114, 131, 132, 145, 146, 151, 153, 154, 155, 157, 159

Eric Strachan: 10, 11, 12, 13, 15, 16, 18, 19, 20, 21, 22, 86, 87, 88, 89, 90, 91

Sunroom Company: 70

Joyce R. Wilson: 32, 33, 35, 36, 37, 38, 94, 95, 98, 101, 110, 113, 115, 116, 117, 120, 134, 137, 139, 141, 142, 144, 149, 161, 169, 173, 174

Index